ADVANCE PRAISE FOR

Sista Talk

"Joining well-crafted storytelling to social analysis, Rochelle Brock's introspective inquiry provides an exciting examination of unequal power, race, womanism, alienation, consciousness, and transformation. This is must reading for those who care about learning and the human spirit.

William H. Watkins, Professor of Education, University of Illinois at Chicago,
Author of The White Architects of Black Education

"Rochelle Brock, feeling that she has 'stood on the shoulders of giants,' has been influenced by the work of African-American scholars such as Patricia Hill Collins, Joyce King, and bell hooks. This book provides the search for Afrowomanist pedagogy by relying on student voices and a slice of autoethnography. Professor Brock reminds us of the power of an emancipatory pedagogy that is critical, Afrocentric, and Black feminist. This book is a must read for educators interested in a critical transformative multicultural education."

Lourdes Diaz Soto, Professor of Education, The Pennsylvania State University

"*Sista Talk* is a journey through the personal and pedagogical. Rochelle Brock stitches together empirical research and action research to present a dialogue about Black women's empowerment. A blend of theory and practice, *Sista Talk* strives to find a pedagogy appropriate for the education of Black students, particularly Black females. Brock has invited her readers to participate in a dialogue that must continue if we are to successfully educate Black children."

Venetria K. Patton, Associate Professor of English
and Director, African American Studies and Research Center, Purdue University

Sista Talk

Studies in the
Postmodern Theory of Education

Joe L. Kincheloe and Shirley R. Steinberg
General Editors

Vol. 145

PETER LANG
New York • Washington, D.C./Baltimore • Bern
Frankfurt am Main • Berlin • Brussels • Vienna • Oxford

Rochelle Brock

Sista Talk

The Personal and the Pedagogical

PETER LANG
New York • Washington, D.C./Baltimore • Bern
Frankfurt am Main • Berlin • Brussels • Vienna • Oxford

Library of Congress Cataloging-in-Publication Data

Brock, Rochelle.
Sista talk: the personal and the pedagogical / Rochelle Brock.
p. cm. — (Counterpoints; vol. 145)
Includes bibliographical references.
1. Afro-American women—Education—Social aspects. 2. Feminism and
education—United States. 3. Critical pedagogy—United States. 4. Brock, Rochelle.
5. Afro-American women teachers—Biography. I. Title.
II. Counterpoints: (New York, N.Y.); vol. 145.
LC2731 .B74   370'.89'96073—dc21   99-088001
ISBN 0-8204-4953-9
ISSN 1058-1634

Bibliographic information published by **Die Deutsche Bibliothek**.
Die Deutsche Bibliothek lists this publication in the "Deutsche
Nationalbibliografie"; detailed bibliographic data is available
on the Internet at http://dnb.ddb.de/.

Cover design by Lisa Barfield

© 2005 Peter Lang Publishing, Inc., New York
275 Seventh Avenue, 28th Floor, New York, NY 10001
www.peterlangusa.com

Printed in the United States of America

To my Black sisters throughout the Diaspora who are struggling to find that safe space that allows them to BREATHE I dedicate this book.

— For Roberta —

Contents

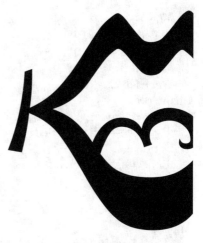

Preface
   Right Words, Wrong Words by Shirley Steinberg   ix
Shout Outs   xi
I Am   xiii
Prologue
   Crossing the Bridge with Lessons I've Learned   xv

Transition
   A War with Words   1
Chapter One
   Theories of the Other: Resistance and Acceptance
   Rising from the Ashes—Engendering an Understanding
   of Black Women and Me   5
Reflection
   scrambled eggs over mediun   20
Chapter Two
   A Conversation with My Goddess Oshun:
   A Theoretical Framework in the Making..   21
Transition
   My Manifesto of Education   29
Chapter Three
   We Said It: The Method to Our Madness   31
Reflection
   SILENCE   37
Chapter Four
   Sista to Sista to Sista: A Story in Three Acts   41
Reflection
   "I really don't breathe, that's part of my problem"   75

Chapter Five
    A Pedagogy of Wholeness:
    Part One—The Theory 83
Transition
    Michael 101
Chapter Six
    A Pedagogy of Wholeness:
    Part Two—The Practice 105
Transition
    Reflecting on Self 117
Chapter Seven
    The End of My Beginning 119

Appendix A:
    The Methodology of Sista Dialogue: Safe Spaces for Being Us 121
Appendix B:
    The Boring but Necessary Stufff 129

References 135

Preface
Right Words, Wrong Words
by Shirley Steinberg

How does one preface poetry and art? When the right descriptors aren't there, every sentence feels heavy, clumsy, overblown? What can I add to a book that jumps out at you, grabs your gut, and leaves you better for having met Rochelle? I don't want to be cool, clever, and especially not deep. I don't want to move from the words Ro has given.

My sisterfriend has given us a piece of talking pedagogy, musical teaching, connected and rooted thoughts that take us through her journey of self-discovery. This book is a shout out to all of us who attempt to scrutinize our essence and bare our discoveries, fears, and conquests. With this book, Rochelle has given us her goddess to mentor our own self-discoveries and to teach us how to teach.

— Shirley Steinberg
October, 2004

Shout Outs

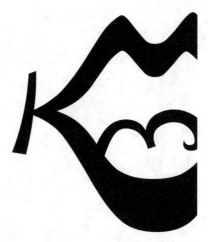

This little book began as my dissertation and ended as what I hope and pray will be useful to Black women everywhere. It's been a long time in completing *Sista Talk* and along the way I have been helped, mentored, and bullied by many wonderful friends and colleagues. How can I adequately thank and acknowledge the countless people who in some way have contributed their time, patience, strength, critique, and spirit so that I could write and bring to a close a part of my life story? The answer is I can't do justice and there will be some I forget to mention by name so I will instead say an overall mega big THANKS to all those friends who have been part of this book—you know who you are.

I express my deepest gratitude to the faculty and staff of African/African American Studies at Pennsylvania State University for sheltering me against the storm while I begin the conceptualization of this book. You provided a home for me during those three years of graduate work and in doing so gave me the strength to persevere.

The students who took my classes in African/African American Studies from 1995–1999 I give a major "shout out." Each and every one of you in some way pushed me a little farther and deeper into understanding what was needed in my pedagogy. It is because of what you taught me about teaching that I was able to become better at my craft.

To the women of Sista Dialogue. Although pseudonyms were used your true voice rings true on every page. I appreciate and love each of you for your time and dedication to my work.

Importantly, I want to thank Joe Kincheloe and Shirley Steinberg who kept the faith in me at times when I could no longer find the faith in myself.

And last, I would like to thank my sisters—three wonderfully strong and beautiful Black women.

"The Brown Menace or Poem to the Survival of Roaches," copyright 1974 by Audre Lorde, from *Collected Poems* by Audre Lorde. Reprinted by permission of W.W. Norton & Company, Inc.

I AM

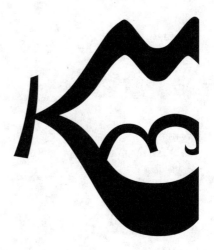

I am
a black woman yes,
I am.
I am not your
chattel mammy jezebel emasculator matriarch sapphire aunt jemima but I am
a

strong.
Black.
Woman.
I am not your
exotic 'other' nor your tall-light skinned-long hair- "I got Indian in my
family" but I am
a
beautiful.
Black,
woman.
I am not your
hoe your trick your bitch the woman that you continually disrespect in your
lyrics but I
am
a loving. Intimate.
Black.
Woman.
I am not your
church going every Sunday-praising the Holy Spirit-seeking freedom after
death but I am
a

spiritual.
Black.
Woman.
I am
a
black.
Woman yes
yes. Yes. Yes. Yes.
Black yes
woman yes yes
black woman yes
I am

Sassy Ross
The African American Woman
Final Class Project, 1998

Prologue
Crossing the Bridge with Lessons I've Learned

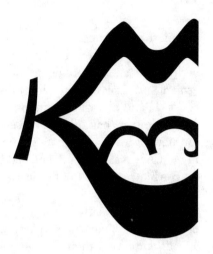

Friends, family, mentors, and enemies constantly accuse me of being an angry Black woman. How do I answer them without becoming even angrier? What words should I string together to make them understand that simply being aware of the historical devaluation of Black women brings anger? Without preaching or sermonizing, how can I tell them that once a Black feminist consciousness is developed a woman has no choice but to see the pain of her sisters and feel her own pain? How do I make them see that even by calling me (and other aware Black women) angry they are accepting the dominant stereotypes of us as aggressive, emasculating bitches? How can I answer any of these questions when all I want to say is, "You will never understand, so get the hell out of my paradigm!"

In her article "Anger in Isolation," Michelle Wallace states, "Being a black woman means frequent bouts of impotent rage" (1995, p. 225). This has become one of my favorite quotes because for me (and others), the rage can often be all encompassing and difficult to work through, with no visible way out. The impotency derives from being just plain "dog tired" of trying to find and maintain a sense of self when people are attempting to take us out of ourselves. I see this in myself and in my young Black female students as they struggle to find a positive *concept of self* in the midst of a confusing and hostile world. I know their struggle because it is also my struggle, one I deal with daily. Sometimes I am able to find the reservoir of strength, but there are days when, regardless of how hard I try, my rage paralyzes. I momentarily accept my otherness/nothingness, and buy into the belief that I can only be what they say I am.

Throughout my teaching career I have agonized over how to better understand myself and use this to more effectively teach my students. And as I work for this understanding, I question, *Where do I begin my journey?* I have been searching for the connection between the personal me as a Black woman and the pedagogical me as a Black woman teacher. How do I marry the two and increase my wholeness in both areas? This has been my constant and consistent battle with myself. As proof, my computer's hard drive is overflowing with papers and proposals on identity, stereotypes, dimensions of disempowerment, *the dozens*, spirituality in pedagogy, Afriwomanist pedagogy in action research, and Black independent education to name a few. Some topics stayed around longer than others and several reemerged periodically throughout my journey toward my ultimate purpose for this book, my life. I "now know" that my journey was African centered in nature; it was not linear but was formed by concentric circles building together and simultaneously narrowing upon the preceding one.

And yet through it all I have continuously analyzed the pain Black women experience living in a society which methodically devalues, dehumanizes, and disempowers them. Simultaneously, I have analyzed my own pain as a Black woman and how that pain has informed my pedagogy. This book is the product of the time I spent teaching courses in African American studies as a graduate student. My classroom became my laboratory, providing the space where I could utilize or discard the theoretical understanding of education and teaching that I was receiving in graduate classes. I understood, even then, that there were three spaces of existence. This abstract concept defines the options I have to help me understand myself.

The first space is where society attempts to imprison me based on my color, class, and gender. I refuse to live there. The second space is where the academy attempts to constrain my knowledge based on my race, class, and gender. I refuse to live there. I worked in the third space of indigenous knowledge, which kept me grounded in my own positionality. It is this space that allows me to put my Black femaleness at the center of the search for knowledge. Here is where I can begin to know myself and Black women by asking and searching for the answers to ontological questions of existence. I place the knowledge created by my Black sisters at the fore. The third space is where I live and learn, stretch and breathe.

I bring myself into this subject completely. I combine and ferret out the previous topics and concerns to realize that all the time I have been seeking an understanding of how I *deal* with my Black femaleness and what this knowledge means to *my* pedagogy. The dialectics of life frame my journey within. In order to appreciate my teaching philosophy I must know myself as a Black woman. Simultaneously, to gain this knowledge, I must be aware of my Black female students as they search and reach for deeper self-knowledge.

My positionality insisted that I become aware of self. Yoruba priestess Iyanla Vanzant (1995) observes in *The Value in the Valley: A Black Woman's Guide through Life's Dilemmas* that *awareness* is the value in the Valley of Light. As my students say, I feel her words:

By reflecting on ourselves and our experiences, accepting what we see, making choices and changes without fear or resentment, we become aware. Awareness enables us not only to know a thing exists in us, but also able to recognize how it operates. When we know who we are, we become aware of how we function. When we are aware of how we function, we are not ready and willing to accept what people say about us. The true value of awareness is that it provides us with courage and strength to resist those people and conditions that do not reflect the true image of who we are. (p. 77–78)

I seek awareness. Awareness of myself as a Black woman. Awareness of myself as a teacher. Awareness of how I join the two. I am taking a journey into myself and my struggles as I search for a transformative way of being and teaching. For me, it is through teaching that awareness has come to *visit*. It only *visits* because daily I have to find the hidden message—that which ideology blurs and mystifies. As soon as I become comfortable with my existence, take a breath, relax, I am reminded that I must wage a *constant* struggle and search for meaning. The ability to read the world is a strategy for survival for those of us who live at the margins of society.

I have spent the majority of my life in the depths of the valley, blanketed in a depression, which effectively blocked out any light. There was a time when I believed that what I was living through was my destiny and it was senseless to expect or hope for anything different. I was able to find my way out of the depression, reenter life through learning and teaching and with that reentry I am able to practice a transformative teaching by way of my understanding of the human experience.

This book is about awareness, both mine and that of young Black women. Throughout these pages (and my life) I ask, "How do Black women analyze the internal dialectics and dichotomies of life?" Webster defines dichotomy as the state of being divided in two. W.E.B. Dubois (1903), in all of his wisdom, wrote about two warring souls that live inside of African Americans. For Black women, dichotomies are the either/or positions we hold in society and they provide the space for stereotypes of Black women to exist. I am at the same time specifically a Black woman with a Ph.D. and generally a Black woman who must battle the perception of me as less than that. Dialectics is the broader arena in which dichotomies thrive and is defined as the unity and struggle of opposing forces that happen simultaneously. It is in the dialectics and dichotomies that Black women search for truth and a deeper meaning of existence. The internal dialectics of Black women are the strength we have historically shown in the face of insurmountable odds as well as our acquiescence to a hegemonic force, which devalues, degrades, dehumanizes, and kills. We are simultaneously strong and weak and in order to understand Black women, one must discover both sides of the dialectic.

In understanding both sides of the internal dialectics of Black women I am led to ask how Black women both accept and fight their status as *other.* The triple binds of race, sex, and class which Black women live within create us as the *other*. The dialectics of Black women engender an internal struggle against being *othered*, as well as accepting their *otherness*. An abstract concept like the *other* becomes reified as a constant battle is waged to remove and guard against existence as the *other*. We internalize the devaluation of Black women through the ideological constructs of thought and action. How we are portrayed becomes natural—we see, hear, and feel that which devalues Black women so much that it seeps into your being and festers, generating anger and exhaustion as we fight. I *need* to understand the forms of resistance and acceptance young Black women enact against this reified *other*.

In spite of—and because of—the dichotomies and dialectics, as well as the possibility of accepting self as *othered*, Black women can reach a positive image of womanhood. What is the process toward this maturation into self-identity? What are the opposing forces Black women struggle against in their rise to a social/political consciousness? For my own sanity I must find the answer to how Black women become socially aware and mature into their self-identity. These areas are intimately connected and serve as the guidepost to understand how Black women make meaning of their life.

The motivating force behind my introspection is that it is about me and my attempt to understand self. This is about self-discovery, a Black woman consciousness, and the lived pedagogy of my students and myself. I am inevitably a part of my own study. I cannot allow this book to slip into an objectified treatise on Black women. As a Black woman in America, I know firsthand how society can shape and construct one's personality and self-perception. I also realize how others view me can influence my view of self. My anger resurfaces when I allow the ways I am viewed by society as a Black woman to affect me. Even though intellectually I realize those views are constructed, emotionally they affect how I feel about myself.

I search for an understanding of self and Black women. And yet at the same time I also need to explore how undergraduate Black female students feel about being Black and female in America. Where do their feelings originate—internally or externally? What do they think were the influences on their sense of identity? How do they identify themselves compared to how others identify them? Is anger a part of their lives, and if it is, how do they deal with that anger? What do these questions and their answers have to do with discovering a pedagogy of humanity and evolving philosophy—creating wholeness in Black women?

I want to understand how Black women make meaning of their lives. I want understand how they accept or reject the images of Black women that are part of America's ideology. I want to understand their acceptance or rejection of these images and how the images manifest themselves in relation to their perceived and received identity. I want to depathologize Black women by examining the conditions of our oppression and once I make sense of that oppression, let it lead to liberation and transformation in self-teaching. My ultimate aim is to lay out the parameters and characteristics of my definition of effective teaching of African American students. I want to understand the symbiotic relationship between my personal and my pedagogical. What are those transitions that have constructed me as teacher and how do they shape my teacher identity?

I am and shall always be a teacher. My career objectives, my academic priorities, and the focus of my life are related to my vision of the world as a place to live, grow, and to create possibilities. Thus, I believe that it is paramount that I constantly strive to enrich my knowledge of pedagogy, sharpen my research skills, and stretch the possibilities that exist for the acquisition and dissemination of learning. I understand teaching as a personal act—I am a teacher who believes in a pedagogy of possibilities because I am a person who understands that despite or because of life's uncertainties, it can have as many possibilities as we allow ourselves to envision.

Yes, my vision. I question my purpose and, more importantly, wonder where the answers will lead us? What can be expected from this journey into *my* oppositional space of existence? Will you want to enter into my paradigm? My life experiences are the harbingers, guiding this study from birth to death. It is these experiences that have predetermined that I write about pain and healing, teaching and oppression, capture and rapture, meaningful transformation, and revolutionary thought. My life forces me to problematize in unconventional ways pain and healing, surf new waters, inquire, investigate, analyze, ruminate, figure shit out, define, refine, and re-remember the story of Black women and me.

As I play with and attempt to figure out this world, I also play with the traditional structure of this book. Throughout its pages you will see the inner dialogue and personal struggles I have being who I am and, more importantly, who I want to become. This inner turmoil, my conversation with self, is situated in double-border boxes, which represents the boxed Rochelle. That piece of me that tries to conform to a standard I'm not even sure about. And yet all the while I am trying to conform I also struggle to break out of and away from those external and internal forces that constrain me. The turmoil lives.

As I wrote and reflected and wrote more, there were words, poetry, songs that at times clarified or troubled my thoughts. These pieces of inblackment float on the pages of *Sista Talk*. I place them around and in between the text because they are that which made the text come alive for me. They are necessary. My life is situated within and defined by them.

I use Reflections and Transitions between chapters to join and pull apart my thoughts, my meanderings. The Reflections are those parts of my past that have played an important part of who I am today. They are me re-remembering the roads I have traveled, at times against my will, to bring me to this place today. The Transitions are the practical connections between the theoretical discussions of chapters.

Occasionally, when needed, I place the voices of my Black female students in single-lined horizontal boxes. I do this when their specific frustrations had an obvious and overt relation to what I was writing at that given moment. Their voices are as central to my attempt to understand as anything. I needed the spirit they offered me as I conceptualized and wrote this book. Throughout I tried to remain true to what they said.

I use Oshun, an African goddess to help me find the strength to tell my story. She is my internal other. The person who pulls me back into some semblance of sanity and clarity. She is my spiritual guide; who I want to become. Dialogue is the central focus of my pedagogy. Dialogue is how I make things clear. The only way I could possibly think my way through the quagmire to write *Sista Talk* was through dialogue and through Oshun.

This book grows out of indigenous research, drawing from scholarship in Black feminist theory, critical theory, critical pedagogy, Afrocentric theory, Black women's literature, poetry, drama, storytelling, and whatever else is needed and valuable. While these separate and discrete areas have influenced me, I do not live in any bounded space. Instead I see myself existing in a liminal space. I am not amorphous, nihilistic, nor am I rejecting traditional paradigms. Instead, I am embracing new epistemological traditions centered in a Black feminist ideology. *Sista Talk* is a contribution to the emerging Afriwomanist discourse of the last few decades.

Please share my journey.

Transition
A War with Words

O nce upon a time there was a society of priests who built a Celestial City with gates secured by word-combination locks. The priests were masters of the Word and, within the City, ascending levels of power and treasure became accessible to those who could learn ascendingly intricate levels of Word Magic. At the very top level, the priests became gods; and because they then had nothing left to seek, they engaged in games with which to pass the long hours of eternity. In particular, they liked to ride their strong, sure-footed steeds around and around the perimeter of heaven, now jumping word hurdles, now playing polo with concepts of the moon and the stars, now reaching up to touch that pinnacle, that splinter of Refined Understanding called Superstanding, which was the brass ring of their merry-go-round.

In time, some of the priests-turned-gods tired of this sport, denounced it as meaningless. They donned the garb of pilgrims, seekers once more, and passed beyond the gates of the Celestial City. In this recursive passage they acquired the knowledge of Undoing Words.

Beyond the walls of the City lay a Deep Blue Sea. The priests built small boats and set sail, determined to explore the uncharted courses and open vistas of this new terrain. They wandered for many years in this manner, until at last they reached a place that was half a circumference away from the Celestial City. From this point the City appeared as a mere shimmering illusion, and the priests knew that they had finally reached a place Beyond the Power of Words. They let down their anchors, the plumb lines of their reality, and experienced godhood once more.

Under the Celestial City, dying mortals cried out their rage and suffering, battered by a steady rain of sharp hooves whose thundering, sound-drowning path described the wheel of their misfortune.

At the bottom of the Deep Blue Sea, drowning mortals reached silently and desperately for drifting anchors dangling from short chains far, far overhead, which they thought were lifelines meant for them. (Williams, npn, 1991)*

---

* I tried to write my own story but I could think of none better than this so I must send I big shout out to Patricia Williams—Thank you my spiritual sister.

I take my cup of coffee and relax into a sitting fetal position on my old, tattered sofa. Looking around my crowded living room I sigh praying for a sign that I am not alone in the inner conflict that has recently taken a stronghold on my Being. I pick up a book, one among many I am hoping will lead me into the first pages of this book. My prayers are heard as the ancestors guide my hand to *The Alchemy of Race and Rights* by Sister Patricia Williams. She begins her story with the parable of the Celestial City. Yes. Perfect, I know how she feels in her attempt to "think" and "talk" like a lawyer. I smiled a smile of camaraderie when I read Patricia's words, her thoughts. In the opening pages she brings the reader into her thoughts and the kitchen table at her mother's house as she and her sister discuss their separate lives.

"But what's the book about?" my sister asks, thumping her leg against the chair impatiently.

"Howard Beach, polar Bears, and food stamps," I snap back. "I am interested in the way legal language flattens and confines in absolutes the complexity of meaning inherent in any given problem; I am trying to challenge the usual limits of commercial discourse by using an intentionally double-voiced and relational, rather than a traditional legal black-letter, vocabulary. . .to speak as black, female, and commercial lawyer has rendered me simultaneously universal, trendy, and marginal. I think, moreover, that there is a paradigm at work, in the persistent perception of me as inherent contradiction: a paradigm of larger social perceptions that divide public from private, black from white, dispossessed from legitimate. This realization, while personal, inevitably informs my writing on a professional level. . ."

"What's so new," asks my sister, losing interest rapidly, "about a schizophrenic black lady pouring her heart out about food stamps and polar bears?"

I lean closer to her. "Floating signifiers," I whisper. (Williams, 1991, pp. 6–7)

My inability to think stays with me. Try as I might I cannot seem to get a handle on the confusion and inadequacies that have taken hold. How do I get through this? How do I use strings of words to relate the string of stories that are inside?

I want my language to be three dimensional, not confined by the flat space of a piece of paper. I want my language to tell a story, but not become objective speech about someone else, someone removed from me. Instead, language is personal and needs to bring forth the personal stories it is trying to relate to the reader. Words should be shaped and molded to your needs. Still the question remains, How can I use a language that is more meaningful, but less academically accepted?

Theories of the Other:
Resistance and Acceptance

Rising from the Ashes—
Engendering an Understanding of
Black Women and Me

Ingredients to make a goddess:
- spirit of ancestors
- a healthy dose of angst
- sense of humor
- patience
- theoretical understanding of all and everything
- excellent eyesight (when you are tired from staring at the computer for 10 hours straight)
- wholeness of being

Take your ingredients and stir while listening to your favorite jazz tune—preferably Cassandra Wilson. Allow the sounds of a Black woman to seep into your mixture. When everything is smooth (the mixture, not the jazz) get out your old beater and slip a pumpin', bumpin' reggae CD in, turn it up as loud as you can and twirl and dance as you beat the shit out of your mixture—remember, you are paying homage to those who came before, so do it with the rhythm of your past—the faster the better.

And call her Oshun, the African goddess of voluptuous beauty, the goddess of love, the goddess of fertility, the female master of strategy. Oshun is the sweet and sour taste of life.

A goddess was just what Rochelle needed. Not only a higher power but one from the historical memories of an African past. Created with music and brought to life with rhythm and soul, a goddess with the strength to move the paradigm beyond the margins. She holds a golden chain in her hands, a chain to tie all of her people together.

Together Oshun and Rochelle will write and speak their truth. Oshun brings voice to the silence surrounding Rochelle. Rochelle brings life to the historical memory of Oshun. As one they tell a Black woman's story.

I have been drowning in the bowels of the Celestial City. I was let into the City of Words, but only so my Words could be mocked, deemed as unimportant, inconsequential to the larger scheme of Superstanding. I was confused and stuck, not even knowing how to write a facile sentence in a language not meant for me. I was fighting an abstract, stubbornly refusing to engage with something that felt alien.

Why?

My head hurts, I cannot fill my lungs up with enough air to speak a thought, even one that is silent. I need to turn away, take a mind rest, at least for a moment, from this malaise. But I can't. It is too important to work my way through, process my alienation from abstract thought, explain and articulate so you can understand. My purpose is to write about a liberating pedagogy for African American women, one that goes beyond critical pedagogy. I want to delve into the secrets of Black women's epistemology—how they define it but not as some third-party, "objective" observer. I've termed it "Afriwomanism," which will provide the critical lens through which I cast my gaze. But the pieces will not come together in a cohesive puzzle. Instead, I sit in my office alternately drinking coffee and coke, killing myself with cigarettes, questioning my intelligence or ability.

Why!

OSHUN: Do you recall the words Gloria Yamato (1995) wrote in "Something about the Subject Makes It Hard to Name?" She called racism, and all of its manifestations, a mind-funk that distorts thought and action (p. 71). My sisterfriend Yamato continues in her explanation of racism by positing that internalized racism is what gets in her way as a Black woman:

> It influences the way I see or don't see myself, limits what I expect of myself or others like me. It results in my acceptance of mistreatment, leads me to believe hat being treated with less than absolute respect, at least this once, is to be expected because I am Black, because I am not white. (p. 73)

Yes. A mind-funk, caused by internalized racism, had encapsulated my thoughts, my entire sense of being until I could not find the words to articulate the things I knew. I realized I had become theoretically challenged, not by outside forces but from the inside. I had allowed the words of others to enter my Being, forgotten that those *drifting anchors dangling from short chains far, far overhead, were not lifelines meant for me.* How do I fight against this internalization, this mind-funk? Where is my shelter against the *steady rain of sharp hooves whose thundering sound* describes my pain? My confusion, anger, and isolation increase as I realize that my critical insight into the constructions of Black womanhood does not insulate me from the daily pain of my otherness. But then perhaps if I did not possess a critical understanding, I would be crazy rather than terminally depressed.

I don't know.

OSHUN: My sisterfriend, don't you see that racism works at the decomposition of the cultural integrity of Blackness (Murrell, 1997)? Decomposition, the breaking into parts, affords a visual, emotive sensation to describe the realities of racism. To remain whole, a person must keep a constant vigil against internalizing racism. Anything short allows the space to exist where mind-funk can thrive. More than a catchy phrase, mind-funk is a consuming way of reading the world and reading the self. It fosters the doubt that stops a person from moving beyond their prescribed boundaries. This mind-funk has enveloped your soul; it's taken away your wholeness. You are *defining* yourself through it, accepting your worth based on the classifications, Black and woman; you have unnecessarily limited your options. You are forgetting your own power of thought. You were not careful enough, not cognizant enough; you waited a minute too long before affixing your armor.

ROCHELLE: Yes, yes, I know, but still this positionality as Black and female hinders the ability I need to think my way out of this oppressive frame of mind. I keep thinking to myself, "You're a poor colored girl. You are not meant to be writing a book!" I laid down my armor because I was just so damn tired of constantly having to hold it. I thought I could take a vacation for a minute. . . .

OSHUN: And I guess you found out that there is no mental vacation.

ROCHELLE: Which is so unfair. But I also found out that there were some larger questions I needed to ask about how this decomposition both manifested itself and how or what I needed to do to resist it. How does racism accomplish the decomposition of the cultural integrity of Blackness? How can I develop and then become a critical pedagogue and ameliorate the transformation of students into critical cultural agents? Why am I allowing myself to be silenced and not using the critical thinking skills I have? Moreover, how do I help my African American students re-remember the spiritual strength that aided our ancestors during the years of capture, enslavement, colonization, and exploitation?

OSHUN: Spiritual strength. Yes. Re-remembering and reconnecting with that which aided our ancestors is extremely important to your survival and the strength you need. Tell me, what gets in your way, hinders you as a Black woman?

ROCHELLE: Concepts of me as the other. A nonentity.

Object/Subject and the *Other*

> My position and that of Black women in America is as the *other*. Such a strange term to describe a person. What does being the *other* have to do with how I feel about myself? The explanations of others, their writings and musings, I occasionally allow (if I am not careful) to seep into my thoughts. Yamoto calls it a mind-funk. I need to think of my own word. But can a word or phrase accurately capture, so others can understand, what can happen to a person's soul when they have to fight constantly for their humanity? "Struggle" and "survival" are too limiting; they still denote a mere existence. But life is more than existence or at least it should be.

OSHUN: The decomposition of the cultural integrity of Blackness is cultivated, in part, through an ideology of the *other*.

ROCHELLE: This I understand, but still it affects me. When I disrobe, lay down my shield, rest, I am left with no choice but to use my *otherness* to define the boundaries of my existence. As the *other* I am removed, standing at the perimeters of normalcy helping to clarify a criterion I can never meet.

OSHUN: Yes, and once you realize and accept those falsehoods you can begin to recreate yourself. The *other* is a paradoxical relationship that "threatens the moral and social order," as well as being "essential for its survival because those individuals who stand at the margins of society, [also] clarify its boundaries" (Collins, 1991, p. 68). African American women, by not belonging, emphasize the significance of belonging.

Being the other means feeling different; is awareness of being distinct; is consciousness of being dissimilar. It means being outside the game, outside the circle, outside the set. It means being on the edges, on the margins, on the periphery. Otherness means feeling excluded, closed out, precluded, even disdained and scorned. It produces a sense of isolation, of apartness, of disconnectedness, of alienation. (Madrid, 1988, p. 12)

OSHUN: Think about ideology. How society thinks of itself, how it knows itself. When we discuss the concept of ideology we are talking about social consciousness. It is the framework people use to make sense of the world, to understand their culture, know what to believe in and then act on that belief. Ideology allows and enforces the constructions of Black womanhood to be taken for granted and implies some natural state, because what is forgotten, and ignored, is that images of Black women are faulty constructions of reality, created by dominant thought, as much as it creates dominant thought. It is so devious, the ways in which ideology functions.

ROCHELLE: Devious, what do you mean?

OSHUN: Look at you. Rochelle, you teach your students about ideology and oppression every day yet right now, at this moment you cannot see the ideological constructs that are holding your mind hostage. It's a hidden, four-pronged attack, coming at you from all sides. Most of us go through life completely unaware of the forces that have constructed our lived world. Black women have been controlled with an ideology of domination, through legitimization, reification, mystification, and acquiescence, that ideology has used to subjugate, objectify, and dominate Black women in America since enslavement (Collins, 1991; hooks, 1989; King, 1995). First, through legitimization systems of domination are represented as being worthy of support. Likewise, systems of domination are denied or obscured and unequal social relations are hidden. In other words, ideological forces attempt to ensure that oppressed people are either not aware of their own oppression or aware but not necessarily able to articulate it (Kincheloe & Steinberg, 1997). Second, through reification a transitory state is represented as if it were permanent, natural, or transhistorical. Ideology allows society to believe that the constructed images are valid. Such images are interwoven and occur simultaneously in the continued devaluation of Black womanhood through the use of controlling images.

The ideological dimensions of the power blocs of White supremacy, patriarchy, and class elitism function to control Black women (and others who are *different*). A white supremacist ideology places blackness and femaleness at the bottom and itself at the top, in power.

Ideology works vis-à-vis fragmentation which occurs when meaning is fragmented and groups and individuals are placed in opposition to each other. This allows for visions of Black women as abnormal through dichotomous thinking, which categorizes based on difference. This binary opposition uses women to define men, nature to define culture, good to define evil, black to define white, as each part of the binary gains meaning only in relation to its counterpart. Dichotomous thinking becomes the ideological tool used in the domination and oppression of Black women by Western society (hooks, 1989) in which things are defined in terms of their difference: they are fundamentally contradictory entities related only through their definitions as opposites. Since these oppositional terms are not equal, they can be defined by the push and pull they create and are resolved by the subordination of one half of the dichotomy to the other. In more concrete terms, not only are Black women defined by their fundamental distinction from men (Black men included) but they have been subordinated to all men based on their gender difference. The patriarchal nature of White supremacy predetermines the subordination. This is the third way in which ideology functions—what is there is mystified, we are constructed not to see the fragmentation.

ROCHELLE: And ultimately it leads to a disparity in economic and cultural capitol. If what I bring to the table (as a Black woman) is deemed insignificant then it holds little or no capital in the struggle for justice and equality.

OSHUN: You got it. Finally, when we are not aware of the forces that attempt to construct and destruct our being, we run the risk of acquiescing to those very forces, becoming that which ideology tells us we are.

> call me
> roach and presumptuous
> nightmare on your white pillow
> your itch to destroy
> the indestructible
> part of yourself.
> (Lorde, 1974, p. 48)

ROCHELLE: It's hard as hell being a Black woman in this society.

OSHUN: As Black women we become "otherized" through binary opposition and are viewed as an object to be manipulated and controlled. Domination always involves attempts to objectify the subordinate group. As the object or subordinate half in a dichotomy, control over how you are defined and represented is usurped by outside hegemonic forces that determine meaning from the very images the dominant group construct. I sent you a book by the author bell hooks where she says that "[A]s subjects, people have the right to define their own reality, establish their own identities, name their history. As objects, one's reality is defined by others, one's identity created by others, one's history named only in ways that define one's relationship to those who are subject" (1989, p. 42).

Being the other involves a contradictory phenomenon. On the one hand being the other frequently means being invisible. Ralph Ellison wrote eloquently about that experience in his magisterial novel *The Invisible Man*. On the other hand, being the other sometimes involves sticking out like a sore thumb. What is she/he doing here? (Madrid, 1988, p. 120)

ROCHELLE: Yes, I remember the book and I remember that statement. But I ask, even as I define self, what of the definition of others? Those definitions are more than just words, they greatly influence the reality I exist within. Don't they?

If one is the other, one will inevitably be perceived unidimensional; will be seen stereotypically; will be defined and delimited by mental sets that may not bear much relation to existing realities. There is a darker side to otherness as well. The other disturbs, disquiets, discomforts. It provokes distrust and suspicion. The other makes people feel anxious, nervous, apprehensive, even fearful. The other frightens, scares. (Madrid, 1988, p. 120)

OSHUN: In order to exercise power, structures of domination in society, i.e., all forms of media, popular culture, schooling, government, etc., utilize existing images of Black women or create new ones to fulfill their needs. A system of domination can be seen in the representations and controlling images of Black women. These images impersonate an outside imposed identity and are shaped by dominant society so as to make racism, sexism, and poverty appear as a natural, inevitable part of life as well as help to maintain interlocking systems of race, class, and gender oppression (hooks, 1981, 1989). The tools of oppression are used by society to exclude Black women, and ideology allows the belief that the constructed images are valid. Moreover, dominant ideology makes it possible that Black women not only internalize, but also become, these created images. In other words we acquiesce.

For some of us being the other is only annoying; for others it is debilitating; for still others it is damning. Many try to flee otherness by taking on protective colorations that provide invisibility, whether of dress or speech or manner or name. Only a fortunate few succeed. For the majority, otherness is permanently sealed by physical appearance. For the rest, otherness is betrayed by ways of being, speaking or of doing. (Madrid, 1988, p. 12)

ROCHELLE: How can I negotiate between my identity as Black and as a woman? I constantly feel torn as to which struggle I align myself with.

OSHUN: It's difficult. Okay, let me situate you in history; in your story. Critical thinking forces you to contextualize your existence. As such, you need to view yourself through the lens of race, class, and gender. It's difficult as hell to negotiate all of our identities, especially race and gender. You must understand the need to fight in the war against racism as well as sexism and at the same time also realize we are often forced to choose between the two. Black women's struggles have been framed within a false dichotomy of race and sex. Often required to choose between the fight against race or gender oppression,

Black women have to constantly reassert the need for a combined struggle. Black women encounter a triple jeopardy where they must constantly negotiate the intersection of race, class, and gender oppression which has forced them into a desperate struggle for existence and a "space" where the freedom to exhale is possible (Hills-Collins, 1991; King, 1995; Wade-Gayles, 1984).

Some time ago I read a wonderful explanation of this triple bind I'm talking about that might help you visualize. Okay, this is how Wade-Gayles (1984) explains it. Picture three concentric circles, each distinctively smaller than the one it is within. The circle which consumes and encapsulates the others is the large space of power where White men, and to a lesser degree White women, experience varying degrees of domination and control and is seen in the systems and structures of society. Sexism, an integral ingredient in understanding relations of power and privilege in America, determines that although White women function within this power discourse of men they are seen as powerless because of gender which becomes the bind of sexism. Within this space is a significantly smaller circle; the place where Black people experience pain and isolation. But also it is the place where Black men live, and although controlled by racism, it still offers a degree of control and provides Black men with the tools to oppress Black women. Denied the power and the privileges of White women, White men, and Black men, Black women are imprisoned in a narrow space of race and a dark enclosure of sex which has engendered a web of pain where Black women strive for the right to *BE*. Of course the binds of class exists in the three circles and their effects are experienced differently depending on race and gender.

ROCHELLE: That's it. There are moments when the reality of my Black femaleness smothers, closes me in.

OSHUN: It is difficult to separate race from class from sex oppression because in our lives they are most often experienced simultaneously. For example, I am not poor today, a woman tomorrow, and Black the following day, but a poor Black woman each day I breathe. A Black woman's existence—how she understands her life—is framed within those three critical domains and to ignore one is to mystify all the others. In order to understand your existence as a Black woman you need to be aware of the myriad forms of power.

ROCHELLE: We are engulfed in a constant struggle between the structures of race, gender, and class causing us as Black women to wage an eternal war against a racist, capitalist, patriarchal society. Clearly, groups are given or denied power based on race, sex, and class in America. Hence, Black women experience triple jeopardy in a white capitalist patriarchal society which requires racial oppression alongside sexual and class oppression (Collins, 1991; hooks, 1989; King, 1995).

My race, class, and gender intertwine to make me who I am. And my consciousness of these three domains constructs every aspect of my identity, including my identity as a teacher. When I teach my students about Black women through the lens of Black feminism I attempt to foster their understandings of the forms ideology has assumed to construct the identity of Black women.

OSHUN: Construct how? Are you being deterministic?

ROCHELLE: My words, thoughts are not meant to take the power of individual Black women away. I don't mean to trivialize or essentialize Black women's reality. I realize that there are powerful ideological justifications for race, class, and gender oppressions (Collins, 1991). Okay, side bar here. My students always pick on me because I have these concepts that I hit them over the head with in class. My favorite mantra is the intersection of race, class, and gender. I force them to look at everything—and I mean everything—through race, class, and gender. These three major concepts intersect under the umbrella of patriarchy, which defines, shapes, and constructs the forms of domination where African American women live. Hegemony's ideological control has manifested itself in various forms including—but not limited to—images that chisel a Black woman's identity as mammy, matriarch, sapphire, Jezebel, and the welfare mother. These are the archetypes of Black female construction and are shaped by dominant society so as to make racism, sexism, and poverty appear as a natural, inevitable part of life.

OSHUN: So how do you understand control?

ROCHELLE: Stereotypes of Black women are interrelated, socially constructed, controlling images, each reflecting the dominant group's interest in maintaining Black women's subordination. These cultural stereotypes are designed to legitimize the causes of and reasons for Black women's oppression. The controlling images help to maintain interlocking systems of race, class, and gender oppression and are tools that serve to mystify societal structures created to achieve the legitimization of oppression. Creating a certain ideology is the tool case that society works with. The purpose and goal of Black feminist thought is to analyze these various ideologies and their many manifestations.

The stereotypes of Black women fall within either/or dichotomous thinking. The four areas through which ideology occurs—legitimization, reification, mystification, and acquiescence—can be seen in the object and subject relations of the various controlling images. This oppositional space between object and subject manipulates the struggle between mind and body and culture and nature (Collins, 1991). When Black and White women are placed within this framework, Black women necessarily are positioned on the side seen as less. Likewise, in a racist, sexist, patriarchal society the group that is constructed as lower will be placed on the subject side of the dichotomy. In a race–sex dichotomy Black women were constructed to represent sexuality unleashed to the true womanhood of White women. As such, the stereotypes of Black women controlled not only Black but White women as well.

OSHUN: Of course you realize that although stereotypes of Black women may change, the underlying ideology of domination remains as an enduring feature of race, gender, and class oppression. Collins (1991) points out that deconstruction allows us to see the ideological and cultural constructs of a concept. We no longer assume that the concept is a simple reflection of reality. The process of deconstructing the "place" of African American women has as its aim or ultimate goal the demystification of the various ideologies that encapsulate Black female identity. In my reality the purpose of Black feminist thought is to place in a contextual framework the philosophies relative to the various systems of control enacted on Black women in America. Deconstructing the negative images of Black women affords an understanding of the genesis and maintenance of those images through the context of race, class, and gender oppression. Now if we place these within an ideological framework, it produces an understanding of the connection between stereotypes, ideology, and African American women. Even more central to the ideology of domination is how those controlling images of Black womanhood take on special meaning because the authority to define these symbols is a major instrument of power (Collins, 1991). Taking away the controlling images is not enough. Socialized into a system that daily teaches you to believe less in your humanity and more in your "nothingness," control and oppression can come from internal as well as external forces.

ROCHELLE: I know. Ideology, domination, control, power, dichotomous thinking, continued devaluation of Black womanhood, subordination, objectification, and controlling images are just a few of the ingredients that dominant social forms use to achieve the decomposition of the cultural integrity of Blackness. I have two choices. I can either acquiesce and accept or resist and change.

At the bottom of the Deep Blue Sea, drowning mortals reached silently and desperately for drifting anchors dangling from short chains far, far overhead, which they thought were lifelines meant for them. Where is my lifeline? How can I effectively articulate the subjugated knowledge that is said to be mine? Needing some type of validation, someone to understand my mind-funk, I began ransacking my bookshelf, searching for writings by Black women, filtering through their stories for insight into what I was feeling.

OSHUN: It can be so easy to acquiesce, to give up. But Rochelle, you come from strong women. Black women have a long-standing tradition of resisting being defined by and through societies' portrayals (Giddings, 1998, 1995; Collins, 1991; hooks, 1989, 1993; White, 1985). Perhaps the "cult of true womanhood" was created to construct women, thereby constructing Black women as an undesirable, unattractive, un. . . . During that same time, Black women were working within their own framework of what it meant to be a woman. Although the "cult of true womanhood"* (Riley, 1986; Welter, 1978) did affect the lives of some Black women, many were still able to usurp that definition to one that was grounded in reality and the struggle of the Black community.

For example, Maria Stewart, the first American woman to lecture in public on political issues, challenged the negative stereotypes of Black women. In 1831 she stated:

> Until union, knowledge and love begin to flow among us. How long shall a mean set of men flatter us with their smiles, and enrich themselves with our hard earnings; their wife's fingers sparkling with rings, and they themselves laughing at our folly? Until we begin to promote and patronize each other. . .Do you ask, what can we do? Unite and build a store of your own. . .Do you ask where is the money? We have spent more than enough for nonsense, to do what building we should want. (as cited in Collins, 1991, p. 238)

Lucy Laney, an ex-slave, insisted that educated Black women must uplift the race and that schools go beyond academic training and address the needs of the community (McCluskey, 1997, p. 405). Nannie Helen Burroughs also refused to fall into either the "cult of true womanhood" or the negative, devalued stereotypes of Black women. Establishing the first all-female school for Black women outside of the South, Burroughs told her students that "No one will give you a chance, you have to take a chance," further using the school motto of "We specialize in the wholly impossible" (as cited in McCluskey, 1997, pp. 417–419).

The examples of Black women fighting against stereotypical images are too numerous to name, but they show a tradition of Black women using various forms of resistance. We can control how racism and sexism affect us. Vanzant states:

> Racism and sexism in and of themselves are not what limit Black women in America. It is our perception of them and how they can or will operate against us that gives them so much power over us. . . . When Black women are taught to be the thing we desire, rather than to see external authorization and approval to have what we desire, O. P. P. [other peoples property] will loose ground in our minds. (1995, p. 194)

---

* Nineteenth-century ideology stated that women were to be "pious, pure, domestic, and submissive," which was incongruous with the realities of life for African American women.

ROCHELLE: We have historically fought the various forms of oppression. Black women also worked to redefine the sexual image society had of Black women as the unsexed, unattractive Mammy or the overly sexed and still unattractive Jezebel. For example, the Black women who sang the Blues during the early 1900s turned both of these images around by creating themselves as sensual, attractive, strong *women* (Davis, 1998). They gave voice to issues concerning Black women, walking and talking in their own paradigm. Independent, strong, assertive, weak, and dependent, the Blues women shed light on the complexities and dialectics of Black women. Being a Black woman did not fall into the "Black woman as pathological and monolithic" framework. Black women have always offered an alternative view to the patriarchal images perpetrated by White society.

OSHUN: Again a unifying theme for our discussion is Patricia Hill Collins. She asserts that Black feminist thought furnishes the space for voice and a self-defined Black woman's standpoint by challenging prevailing approaches to studying oppressed groups. The notion exists that the oppressed identify with the powerful and are seen as less human and intellectual and therefore less capable of interpreting their own oppression. Specifically, Black women's histories have been discussed and analyzed (often incorrectly) by White and Black men, as well as White women who have too often ignored the influence of race, class, and gender on the experiences of Black women. Ann duCille, (1994), raises the question,

> What does it mean for the future of black feminist studies that a large portion of the growing body of scholarship on black women is now being written by white feminists and by men whose work frequently achieves greater critical and commercial success than that of the black female scholars who carved out a field in which few "others" were then interested? (p. 5)

ROCHELLE: My answer is that we (Black women) must continue researching and writing our own histories and critically engage in dialogue with those who attempt to usurp our voice. The authority to define and frame the issues of Black women engenders power over Black women. In contrast, a theory that not only sets out to redefine the standpoint of Black women, but that is also conceived by Black women, serves to better articulate a Black feminist consciousness. Black feminist thought, and by extension a Black feminist epistemology, provides and augments a theoretical understanding of the intersection of race, class, and gender and how they are part of a single, historically created system (Collins, 1991).

The temporary dissipation of my fog again gathered bringing on the inner doubts and questions. My muse was laughingly hiding, offering clues and waiting for me to play Columbo and piece together the disparate thoughts floating above, just out of reach. The ancestors were by my side, offering divine intervention as I attempt to negotiate an unholy alliance with my muse. In their infinite wisdom they guided me to a statement in "Postmodern Blackness" in which hooks (1990) states:

> It is sadly ironic that the contemporary discourse which talks the most about heterogeneity, the decentered subject, declaring breakthroughs that allow recognition of otherness, still directs its critical voice primarily to a specialized audience, one that shares a common language rooted in the very master narratives it claims to challenge. If a radical postmodernist thinking is to have a transformative impact then a critical break with the notion of "authority" as a "master over" must not simply be a rhetorical device, it must be reflected in habits of being, including styles of writing as well as chosen subject matter. (p. 2)

I'll Run My Way Out of This: Healing My Otherness

ROCHELLE: "We are the weavers of our future's tapestry; we and no others" (Hayes, 1995, p. 48). How beautiful and true are these words, but where do we find the threads with which to weave a future of hope? If we are not careful, these can become hopeless times; times where we are afraid to dream, afraid to speak for fear that our words will remain unheard. Even though I strive for knowledge on my otherness; despite my understanding of subjugated knowledge and objectification; regardless of Black feminist thought and critical thinking skills, I still allow myself to be silenced. Does it really matter if that silence is internal or external? I become too tired to make my voice and thoughts heard. Such an insipid thing, racism can seep into every open pore until it fills you with hate and bitterness. I understand the silence and fear students experience in the educational process and I especially commiserate with the psychological abuse Black students deal with on a daily basis. My musings are my attempts to figure out what is going on.

OSHUN: I saw your angst lessen when you placed our discussion of ideology in the abstract. When you stopped trying to relate it to your experiences and began to show how you taught your students about ideology. So is your purpose in all of this to understand you—your students? Are you trying to find or maybe reassert your voice?

ROCHELLE: Umm…my purpose? I guess I am really hoping to figure out my purpose in life. I am trying to connect my personal stories to those of my Black female students. And then I am hoping to connect it, the stories, to my pedagogy, to help me become a better teacher. So these musings are my attempts to figure out what is going on. What does it all mean to me as a critical teacher who is committed to the liberation of oppressed peoples? How does my internal struggle relate to the struggles of the young Black women I choose to study? If I cannot allow my knowledge of the forces that oppress us to help me deal with and get past that mental oppression then how can I help my students do the same? The original problem I experienced with writing and thinking my way through this book is also indicative of the problems I have with the term "critical pedagogy." Something is missing from critical pedagogy, or at least my understanding of the purpose and benefit of this form of pedagogy. I believe for a pedagogy to be truly liberating and empowering for Black students it must involve itself in teaching how to reclaim the spiritual strength of our ancestors. In *Hagar's Daughters*, Hayes asserts that

> It was that knowledge, formed within us as a part of our African heritage, passed down somehow from parent to child, which provided the fire that forged the strength which enabled us to not simple survive, but "move on up a little higher" each time. (1995, p. 16)

Education should provide students "care for their being" with a pedagogy that teaches love of self and others, inner strength, humanity and humanness, survival and struggle, and hope and knowledge. King (1982) declares that "the potential—to exist fully in alignment with one's human spirit—is already present in each of us" (p. 270) and a task of education is "to help us learn hopeful principles of human existence" (p. 273). According to King, Afrohumanity is a soul-freeing liberatory education that nourishes well-being in the individual and helps a person reconnect with their humanity. When education does not provide a person with the right tools to tap into their humanity, it is impossible for hope to survive. A "freeing legacy" in a curriculum of hope and Afrohumanity affords the acceptance of the humanity of everyone without being entangled in the web of proving legitimacy of any individual or group. In contrast to the effects of justifying self, Afrohumanity allows students to see the benefits of engaging with others on an equal basis.

We see our brothers and sisters as human and we understand the urgency in our "getting it together." Finally, we realize and act on the socio-emotional intimacy of sharing in truth seeking and truth speaking amid gender equitableness (p. 273).

I don't have answers to how I would develop and implement such a curriculum; I simply know on a tacit level that the answers are to be found in the past. The women I drew upon to receive the needed validation possessed a spiritual inner strength which was grounded in knowledge of their past. They found ways to believe in the "humanness of self" and survive beyond the boundaries of their otherness. I know I will find the answers to maintain my humanity by appreciating the realities of Nannie Helen Burrows, Zora Neale Hurston, Anna Julia Cooper, the women from the book *We Are Your Sisters*, the bravery and commitment of the members of Student Nonviolent Coordinating Committee, Martin Luther King and Malcolm X, and the countless survivors of the war on African American humanity.

"Stretch or Die" was the call Cherrie Moraga used to end her introduction of *This Bridge Called My Back* (npn). I want to stretch critical pedagogy, Black feminist thought, and my ways of knowing to encompass the past and present so as to create a hopeful future; if not, my silence will bring a death to change and hope of the students I so badly want to help.

I weave a tapestry for the future with threads of hope and humanity.

I will write and think myself away from this. I will prove to me that although critical pedagogy offers insight into the education of Black children it nevertheless does not go far enough for me. Instead, something more is needed, a spiritualness connecting self to something deeper in the education of oppressed peoples. I will combine critical pedagogy with Black feminist epistemology and bring forth a greater truth. Yes.

The mind-funk, the depression, and confusion that had been smothering me for weeks began to open, not completely, just enough so I could see and breathe my way into thought. It was okay to dance with the gods, but instead of the *waltz* I could teach them a funky, rhythmic *cha-cha slide*. I could draft words to define thoughts to tell a story that is both personal and political. Not only can I personalize the political, but I can also politicize the personal. I can do it all while remaining true to *my* voice.

Reflection

scrambled eggs over medium

i remember, it was every wednesday morning. i can't remember for how long, but i know at least for a month, maybe more, i can't remember. they. they served orange juice after it was all over. something about the acid helped, why? i can't remember.

my father would drive me there, as my best friend vicki was walking to school, we were in the ninth grade. no one knew, it was a family secret, a family shame. only the family, the doctors, the nurses, the machine.

i was a fool, i didn't know what they were doing, but then again i was only fifteen, still i was a fool, i should have stopped it. why didn't somebody, any-body. maybe someone did try to stop it, i can't remember.

the volts, they put you to sleep, you didn't feel them, but then again you did in one part of your mind you knew something was different, would never be the same, you felt something. afterwards you would wake. but i remember the sleep also. heavy, dense, grave, shrouded, a sleeping death. i couldn't breath, no air and then i felt emptiness, the deepest nothing, the deepest black hole. i wish i could say i dreamed while i was in the hole, the abyss. but i can't remember.

i remember daddy would wait outside with the other people. i remember a room, a white room with cots. what did the machine look like? i remember small for something that would change my life, forever. where did they hook it to me. what parts of my soul did they try to fry away? did they try to reach that place deep inside where my self lived? it must have been funny to the people in white, seeing me, helpless, without control of me, with things at-tached. i wish i could remember.

what happened once they stopped? where did it all go; what they took away and made me forget? what does it mean for me now, today? how did i return life to self from the ashes? what were my ways of forgetting and remember-ing those wednesday mornings?

A Conversation with My Goddess Oshun

A Theoretical Framework in the Making

OSHUN: A tapestry of hope and humanity. That sounds wonderful.

ROCHELLE: Yes, to remain hopeful is wonderful and it is through teaching that I see that hope. Well not simply see but realize its significance. To me, realizing denotes something more proactive than seeing. There is action in realizing.

OSHUN: Tell me how you are making sense of your study.

ROCHELLE: I am using a variety of assumptions to theorize away the pain of Black women although the main theories will be those developed by African American women scholars for the study of African American phenomena. The first (and perhaps central) framework is Black feminist thought.

OSHUN: Feminist not Womanist?

ROCHELLE: This is going to get confusing now. Black feminist thought is a framework that has been theorized by sisters since the 1970s. These Black women have specifically utilized the phrase "Black feminist thought" and therefore when talking about their theories I, too, use that phrase. Now on another level I use "womanist" and specifically "Afriwomanist" when I write about how I have internalized the concepts and theories of other Black women. I have struggled with the two concepts since I first came into my own Black female consciousness. I have vacillated between the two for several years and just recently I have come to accept "womanist" above "feminist." I listen, I feel, I experience the words of Alice Walker.

Womanist 1. From *womanish*. (Opp. Of "girlish," i.e., frivolous, irresponsible, not serious.) A black feminist or feminist of color. From the black folk expression of mothers to female children, "You acting womanish," i.e., like a woman. Usually referring to outrageous, audacious, courageous or *willful* behavior. Wanting to know more and in greater depth than is considered "good" for one. Interested in grown-up doings. Acting grown up. Being grown-up. Interchangeable with another black folk expression: "You trying to be grown." Responsible. In charge. *Serious*. (Walker, 1983, p. xi)

As a womanist, I immediately position myself in my Black femaleness. This positionality brings forth my self-definition and does not carry the historical baggage embedded in the term feminist.

> **2.** *Also:* A woman who loves other women, sexually and/or nonsexually. Appreciates and prefers women's culture, women's emotional flexibility (values tears as natural counter-balance of laughter), and women's strength. Sometimes loves individual men, sexually and/or nonsexually. Committed to survival and wholeness of entire people, male and female. Not a separatist, except periodically, for health. Traditionally universalist, as in: "Mama, why are we brown, pink, and yellow, and our cousins are white, beige, and black?" Ans: "Well, you know the colored race is like a flower garden, with every color represented." Traditionally capable, as in: "Mama, I'm walking to Canada and I'm taking you and a bunch of other slaves with me.: Reply: "It wouldn't be the first time." (Walker, 1983, p. xi)

As a womanist I am whole, I am strong and proud of my strength. I am aware that I do not have to let that strength define and encapsulate me in a controlling image of "Black superwoman." As a womanist I am centered in Black women's spirit.

> **3.** Loves music. Loves to dance. Loves the moon. *Loves* the spirit. Loves love and food and roundness. Loves struggle. *Loves* the Folk. Loves herself. *Regardless.* (Walker, 1983, p. xi)

As a womanist I develop the power to push the anger away from my being. I find joy in my Black femaleness, my large hips, my rounded butt, my large breasts, my nappy hair, my sexuality, my "attitude," my struggle, my survival, my song, my dance.

> **4.** Womanist is to feminist as purple is to lavender. (Walker, 1983, p. xi)

Womanism is fostered through the multiple identities of Black woman and nurtured in the binds of race, class, and gender oppression (Brown, 1994). When I call myself a womanist ". . . it cannot be said often enough, a womanist is one who loves, who loves deeply, who loves strongly, who loves a community, a people, into being. And this is what we who call ourselves womanist must do" (Hayes, 1995, p. 42). This love takes me further than criticisms of patriarchy into criticisms of all which rob the human race of their humanness.

OSHUN: So you develop your own "politics of epistemology"?

ROCHELLE: Developing an epistemology for the study of Black women is important. I do not need to theorize about myself or the Black women in my focus group using an epistemology that attempts to deny my or their humanity or existence—one which places me as object in my history—without a voice to speak of my realities. Instead, I choose to work within epistemological assumptions grounded in my history as a Black woman. I choose to learn from the all-too-often ignored and silenced theories of Black women regarding how we know and experience our world. A Black feminist epistemology aims to raise the political consciousness of people with an Afrocentric worldview, placing them at the center of their own reality. In addition, a Black feminist epistemology challenges patriarchal structures and gender inequalities (Joseph, 1995).

Working within a Black feminist epistemological framework provides the space to challenge ontological questions of existence and being. How do I understand my realities as an objectified other? Where do I fight the battle for my selfhood? Where is my fight/struggle as a teacher, a scholar, a guide in the journey I take with my students? What can I learn from the historical exploitation of my sisters and how does this knowledge influence/shape my pedagogy? These are all ontological questions asked as I search for the "why" of my Black female self. More importantly, these questions frame the ways the young Black women who were part of my study are attempting to understand the "why" of their existence.

From ontological questions of existence grows a need for an epistemology specific to Black women. Collins (1991) developed a Black feminist epistemology that has four characteristics for understanding African American women. These characteristics are "concrete experience as a criterion of meaning" (pp. 208–212), "the use of dialogue in assessing knowledge claims" (pp. 212–215), "the ethic of caring" (pp. 215–217), and "the ethic of personal accountability" (pp. 217–219).

The first characteristic, "concrete experience as a criterion of meaning" defines two types of knowing—wisdom and knowledge. Wisdom is an important ingredient in African American thought. For example, the person who has knowledge but lacks wisdom is joked about in the Black community. Smitherman (1986) asserts that "from a black perspective, written documents are limited in what they can teach about life and survival in the world. Blacks are quick to ridicule 'educated fools,'. . .they have 'book learning' but no 'mother wit,' knowledge, but not wisdom" (p. 76, as cited in Collins, 1991, p. 208).

This distinction between knowledge and wisdom has been instrumental to Black women's survival. Collins (1991) explains that "experience as a criterion of meaning with practical images as its symbolic vehicles is a fundamental epistemological tenet in African American thought systems" (p. 209). In other words, the concrete is used to assess the abstract because it carries more weight when we can add experience to it. Knowledge allows Black women to understand the interlocking systems of race, class, and gender oppression. Wisdom affords Black women the tools needed to survive in this system and is essential to the survival of those subordinated by hegemonic forces. Wisdom is lived knowledge. Remember my earlier confusion and angst regarding ideology as it personally constructed me? I now see it was grounded in the false separation of knowledge and wisdom. In my mind I knew both sides but my heart, my soul had not joined the two together.

OSHUN: Black women who have never heard of Patricia Hill Collins have nevertheless used and understood the two types of knowing in their struggle toward remaining whole. Collins and others have merely theorized the everyday tacit knowledge of Black women. The heuristic approach to research that you are using places an emphasis on personal knowledge, indwelling, and the tacit dimension, thereby fostering a better understanding of Black women's survival. Patton (1990) states that tacit knowing is the inner essence of human understanding; it is what we know but can't necessarily articulate. Through indwelling we gain access to new and deeper meaning. We understand and experience our knowledge through indwelling, questioning and analyzing self. Patton's description of tacit knowing and indwelling correlates to Vanzant's statement about awareness. When we become cognizant of our indwelling then tacit knowing can be articulated and decoded.

ROCHELLE: The second characteristic of an African American epistemology is the use of dialogue in assessing knowledge claims. hooks (1989) asserts that dialogue implies talk between two subjects, not the speech of subject and object. According to Collins (1991), "a primary epistemological assumption underlying the use of dialogue in assessing knowledge claims is that connectedness rather than separation is an essential component of the knowledge validation process" (p. 212). Connectedness has always been an important part of African American thought, as is evidenced by the assertion that the importance of community outweighs the need of the individual in African American thought. In African American culture this connectedness is related to a sense of being human (Asante, 1991; Asante & Atwater, 1986; Collins, 1991). Asante believes that becoming human or realizing the promise of becoming human is the only task of the person. Collins further states that people become human and empowered only in the context of a community, and only when they "become seekers of the type of connections, interactions, and meetings that lead to harmony" (p. 185). Dialogue allows this to happen.

OSHUN: The dialogue we are in this moment. I talk with you, not to or at you. We know that dialog is an important aspect of African American language. In the African American community, words carry power. Sister June Jordan (1985) posits that,

> Our language is a system constructed by people constantly needing to insist that we exist. . . Our language develops from a culture that abhors all abstraction, or anything tending to obscure or delete the fact of the human being who is here and now / the truth of the person who is speaking or listening. (p. 129, as cited in Collins, 1991, p. 213)

Language is more than words. It cannot be a singular event as in one-sided talk. As the word "dialogue" denotes, an African American epistemology demands discourse. In order for ideas to be tested and validated, everyone in the group must participate. As in the first characteristic which speaks of the importance of community as well as knowledge and wisdom, dialogue occurs within a community of individuals.

Your writing is a dialogue between you and your psyche. You position yourself, with the creation of a goddess and the cute little boxes you have placed throughout, as engaged with and constantly questioning your topic of research. Since I am omniscient I know that where you are now in your thinking is not where you began when you wrote your book proposal or where you will be when you finally let go of the book.

ROCHELLE: This beast has taken on a life of its own and I am being led by forces outside of me to where I need to go.

OSHUN: That's deep.

ROCHELLE: The use of dialogue in assessing knowledge claims supports my methodology, group conversation. Although the study is a three-year self-study of me, my pedagogy, and transformative teaching, the main strategy for data collection was in the form of group discussion. The method of group discussion is "in tune with" the African American tradition of dialogue within a community setting. Rather then relying on individual interviews—a method which is antithetical to Black life—the group discussion method allows data collection in a setting which is more comfortable to many African American women.

The third characteristic of an African American epistemology is the ethic of caring. Collins (1991), asserts that the ethic of caring suggests that "personal expressiveness, emotions and empathy are central to the knowledge validation process" (p. 215). In this way ideas are an integral component of the individuals who create and share them. Furthermore, as in concrete experience, the ethic of caring is also closely tied to connectedness. People are connected to one another through their experience of being human. The aphorism "No man is an island" is appropriate if we use creative license and say "No human is an island who is truly human."

Collins delineates three interrelated components of the ethic of caring. The ethic of caring suggests that "personal expressiveness, emotions, and empathy are central to the knowledge validation process" (Collins, 1991, p. 215). First, the uniqueness of individuals, which is rooted in African humanism, states that each individual is thought to be a unique expression of a common spirit, power, or energy inherent in all life.

OSHUN: And the benefits are what?

ROCHELLE: Individual uniqueness contradicts the definition of monolithic, a description often placed on African American people. Instead, African
Americans, although part of a collective, are unique individuals.

The second component of an ethic of caring is the appropriateness of
emotions in dialogue. Emotion indicates that a speaker believes in the validity
of an argument (Collins, 1991). In African American epistemology, emotion
is recognized as an integral part of Black life. The lived experience of African
Americans in America is one filled with turmoil and strife, yet in spite of this,
and possibly because of it, African American culture is filled with emotion. In
the ways of speech, talk, dress, and thought, being "in touch with your emotions" is a reality for most African Americans. Sister Ntozake Shange states
that one of the goals of her work is to look at how

> Our [Western] society allows people to be absolutely neurotic and totally out of
> touch with their feelings and everyone else's feelings, and yet be very respectable.
> This, to me, is a travesty. . .I'm trying to change the idea of seeing emotions and
> intellect as distinct faculties. (Collins, 1991, p. 216)

OSHUN: Our need for and commitment to emotion has been used against
us; as Black people and as women. We are scorned for our ability to laugh, cry
and shout. Black feminist thought embraces our need for emotions.

ROCHELLE: The third component in an ethic of caring is developing the
capacity for empathy. In other words we share with others when we empathize
with them and they with us. During my time teaching I have developed a close
relationship with my students based on empathy. The students know that I
empathized with their situations and will do what is in my power to help them.
Not to be confused with sympathy, empathy entails an understanding of each
other's positions and not looking on the other person as a victim.

The fourth characteristic of an African American epistemology is the
ethic of personal accountability. Collins (1991) states that African Americans
must develop their knowledge claims through dialogue and present them in a
style proving their connection to their ideas. In addition, African Americans
are expected to be accountable for their knowledge claims. It is essential for
individuals to have personal positions on issues and assume full responsibility
for arguing their validity in the Black community. Views expressed and actions
taken derive from a central set of core beliefs which are personal.

To illustrate this point, Collins (1991) relates a story concerning her students. When discussing an African American male scholar, the students (all
Black women) requested his personal information in their process of assessing
the validity of his knowledge. The students used this information to assess if
the scholar really cared about his topic and drew on this ethic of caring in pro-
cessing their knowledge claims about his work. The students used the person's
concrete life experiences as a criterion of meaning for his worth as a scholar.

They refused to evaluate the rationality of his written ideas without some indication of his personal credibility as an ethical human being.

A Black woman's epistemology works in understanding Black women because it understands/accepts the triple bind of race, class, and sex oppression Black women experience every day they take a breath. Collins (1991) states:

> On certain dimensions Black women may closely resemble Black men; on others, white women; and on still others Black women stand apart from both groups. Black women's both/and conceptual orientation, the act of being simultaneously a member of a group and yet standing apart from it, forms an integral part of Black women's consciousness. Black women negotiate these contradictions, . . . by using this both/and conceptual orientation. Rather than emphasizing how a Black women's standpoint and its accompanying epistemology are different than those in Afrocentric and feminist analysis, I use a Black women's experiences as point of contact between the two. (p. 207)

The four characteristic of an African American feminist epistemology work in relation with one another to aid in the process of understanding Black women. The four characteristics grow out of an Afrocentric approach to the research of and by African Americans. This approach is a dialectical strategy that "aims to help people discover more about their own lives in a culturally relevant way in order to critique their social practice and participate in a changing dominant society" (King & Mitchell, 1995, p. 67). So as to be clear about a confusing term, I am using Afrocentric in the context used by Lerone Bennett (1993) and others which states Afrocentric is a centered perspective or world view that "charges" us with the responsibility to know ourselves and educate ourselves "from the inside" (p. 2–6).

But I have to confess throughout all of this I have constantly questioned and am extremely cognizant of how my knowledge will be viewed, critiqued, analyzed, and dismissed.

OSHUN: The politics of knowledge is a strange animal. Black women have been fighting, struggling, protesting, shouting for decades to have their voices heard and to define a Black woman's intellectual tradition. We have been taking care of our families, our men, our churches, and our communities since even before Ida B. Wells worked to end lynching. We have organized around racial uplift, been politically active even when we couldn't vote, published books and articles about our history, yet the academy and what they take as valid, legitimate knowledge dismisses us at every turn. Even now with the interest in Black women as an object of study, or what Ann duCille (1994) calls "the occult of true black womanhood. . . the traffic jam—that black feminist studies has become" our voices are still being denied (p. 2). duCille questions the politics around the "newfound interest" in Black feminist studies. She answers:

So I have arrived at what for me is at the heart of what's the matter. Much of the newfound interest in African American women that seems to honor the field of black feminist studies actually demeans it by treating it not like a discipline with a history and a body of rigorous scholarship and distinguished scholars underpinning it, but like an anybody-can-play pick-up game performed on a wide-open, untrammeled field. Often the object of the game seems to be to reinvent the intellectual wheel to boldly go where in fact others have gone before, to flood the field with supposedly new "new scholarship" that evinces little or no sense of the discipline's genealogy. (p.10)

Rochelle, my advice to you is to keep doing what you are doing but never forget or ignore those Black women who are the edifice for your own consciousness.

Transition
My Manifesto of Education

What is my philosophy of education? How does it reflect my pedagogical style? How do I understand myself as a teacher? The answers to these questions are constantly changing, growing, because as I learn more about myself, I learn more about my purpose as an educator. I am able to ask the right questions of my students when I am able to ask the right questions of myself. Although there is a common thread, which runs throughout, my philosophy of education is constantly in flux. Of course the more I learn about and experience life, the better able I am to "teach" my students.

I had a discussion with several university colleagues about the concept of "beliefs" and the problem some felt toward that word. Where do I stand? I do hold certain beliefs based on my life assumptions. I also accept that there are certain "facts" and "truths" based on my life experiences. The combination of my beliefs and truths become my philosophy and pedagogy. A truth—The back doors of the educational system are something minority and poor peoples are always fighting to get through. I know that in a system of colonialism, the colonizer has a dual purpose in educating the colonized. The first is socialization into accepting the value system, history, and culture of the dominant society. The second is education for economic productivity. The oppressed are treated like commodities imbued with skills that are bought and sold on the labor market for the profit of capitalists. These things I know as "truths."

I know that we live in a society that judge's people based on their race, class, and gender. That is not a belief but a fact, at least for those who choose to accept it. I know that students who are poor and minority are existing under a system that accepts and promotes their failure. A system that cares little (or nothing) for these expandable cogs in the machinery of capitalism. I know that in most schools, World History equals Western History, children celebrate Thanksgiving by dressing as Indians with art class feather headbands and are told that Columbus discovered America. I know that students of color are hungry for knowledge about their culture (and not add-on teachings of tolerance). I know that Black and Brown children are tracked into "special" classes where they typically remain for the entirety of their school career. I know that the ideology under which America exists constructs these children as nothing and ensures through that construction that these children believe they are nothing. All of these things I know to be real and true and I can never accept a postmodern notion of multiple realities. Not when I *feel* the failure of a large segment of the population. This knowledge leads to my beliefs.

I believe, based on what I know, that as a teacher I must teach all of my students and especially my minority students to think critically, to deconstruct the world. I must provide them with the tools to analyze their everyday life through the lenses of race, class and gender oppression. They must think politically, and see the connections between what they see on a comedy sitcom to what they read or don't read in the newspaper. My pedagogy is educating my students for struggle, survival, and the realization of their humanity. I believe I must teach to demystify the injustices of the world by becoming a radical teacher—facilitating students in the understanding of their self-identity and outside constructed identity, what are the structures working against them, what they must fight, and the form the fight will take—education of self and activism for the community.

How do I go about enacting my truths and my beliefs as they change and I change, although my truths and beliefs manifest themselves differently depending on the needs and identities of my students? What stays constant, and what all my students recognize about Rochelle is that they will leave her class being more aware than when they entered.

As Abraham Lincoln, the great *emancipator*, said, "I hold these truths to be self-evident."

three

We Said It:
The Method to Our Madness

ROCHELLE: My consciousness leads me to question how my Black female students dealt with all of the stuff out there that attempted to silence, subjugate, spiritually kill them.

OSHUN: Okay tell me about it.

ROCHELLE: Well first there was the chili.

ROCHELLE'S CHILI

Ingredients:
Hamburger
Ground Turkey

Sauce:
onions
scallions
several cloves of garlic
red and green peppers
fresh mushrooms
1 tsp white sugar

barbecue sauce
soy sauce
1 tsp lemon juice
1 can of kidney beans
1 large tomato
2 cans of seasoned diced tomatoes
chili powder
mustard

1lb of grated cheese
1cup of diced onions

Before you start cut up all vegetables and set aside. Measurements depend on if you like a lot or a little stuff in your chili. Personally, I like a lot so I used as much of everything as my budget would allow!

Put a portion of cut up onions with meat and brown. Drain off liquid. Note there will be a lot of liquid if you are on a slim budget and buy cheap meat. In a separate pot, combine sauce ingredients. Simmer while meat is cooking. When meat is completely brown (it ruins the data gathering if you give botulism to your participants) combine meat and sauce in a large pot. Season to taste, and let it simmer for two hours while you set up the cameras.

Methodology–Sister Dialogue: An Intellectual Slumber Party*

OSHUN: Girl, your chili is slamming! I don't care what the rest of your focus group was like, what y'all did, talked about, whatever. The chili is good. I don't get food like this in the queendom.

ROCHELLE: Okay, I'm going to essentialize here for a minute. Black women bond around food. There is absolutely no way I can expect a group of Black women to share their souls without serving the only thing I know how to cook well. Me and my girls bonded around food and good conversation for six hours. I held the premise that Black women can be awakened through an Afriwomanist pedagogy of wholeness. I believed that through my teaching philosophy and pedagogy I fostered and guided my Black female students into a new consciousness and sense of who they were. As I have mentioned, my research focused on me and my educational relationship with my students. Specifically since I am doing research on my own community, Black women, I questioned my bias and the impact of my being part of the community of research. To answer I looked at the words of Michelle Foster (1994):

> Many of us are first socialized into the values, norms, and communication standards of our home communities and later, after many years of education, into those of the mainstream culture. Moreover, the subordinate position assigned to our communities in the American social order forces us to see ourselves through others' eyes. This means we are more likely to understand, if only through our own lived experiences, what it means to be marginalized (p. 131).

OSHUN: A researcher who is a member of the community they are researching will not necessarily understand or see everything, but then again research conducted by White researchers on the African American community did not either. As both an insider due to your ethnicity and an outsider due to your age and education, you are required not to place your own beliefs and assumptions on the women in the study.

ROCHELLE: I tried my damndest not to and I must confess it was hard.

OSHUN: At least you are honest.

ROCHELLE: Pedagogy does not just take place in the confines of the classroom and teaching is not a simple nine-to-five job. Black women learn from, and are taught through, a "pedagogy of life" by mothers, othermothers, friends, teachers, the media, family, etc. I appropriated my pedagogy from the classroom and used it to construct a negotiated learning environment–sista dialogue. Sista dialogue comprised a focus group of eight participants which were selected from a pool of my past Black female students. The focus group took place in March, was held at my apartment, and lasted six hours. I have to say that those six hours were intense for all of us.

---

* Please see Appendix A and B for a detailed explanation of the methodology.

OSHUN: I so loved being in your space for *sista dialogue*. Wisdom. Strength. Anger. Questioning. Laughter. The women of *sista dialogue* came together for one evening of sharing what it meant to be Black and female in this society. Your only assumption going into the focus group was that they would talk about anger. What Black woman who is aware of the systems of oppression have you met who is not angry?

ROCHELLE: Seeing your oppression makes you angry and being a critical thinker makes you want to do something about that anger. Besides my one assumption, I did not have a list of planned research questions. Questions and their answers were not my purpose. Instead, I wanted to hear what the women had to say. How they understood their existence. How they made sense of this world. They were all survivors. Why? How did they do it?

I tried not to act as teacher, but as a facilitator, moving the discussion when and if it became stale. But the women wanted answers to their questions. They would not allow me to be an objective observer, dispassionately taking notes. I reentered the role I have played in all of their lives—teacher, mentor, friend, mother. But I did not mind; I relish that role.

OSHUN: What did you find out? Did the group help you come any closer to transformative teaching? Did you learn anything new about being Black and a woman?

ROCHELLE: I think the focus group helped the women more than it helped me. I did not answer any deep and searching questions with the group. I did not unearth any truths, which have not already been discussed by the many Black women who have pondered, theorized, and researched the question of existing as a Black woman. What I did for the women in the group was provide a safe space to discuss their feelings and fears, their wants and desires, what they know to be true and what they are still wondering about.

OSHUN: Yes, that's all well and good, but is that valid and academic?

ROCHELLE: I believe it is. The group was an epistemological journey into how they construct knowledge about self. I used the words "feelings and fears" because emotion was a large part of the evening. That is how they negotiated their understandings of self. We are emotional people and I will not give credence to the dichotomy that places emotion below rational thought (Collins, 1991; hooks, 1994).

As I sat and listened, certain themes emerged from the group which were confirmed when I began to analyze the transcripts. Awareness, self-reflection, a strong sense of family, spirituality, a Black woman's consciousness, commitment to the struggle of Black people and Black women. I chose wisely when I decided these were the women I wanted. And I have to allow myself to feel that in some way my teaching and mentorship acted as a catalyst to put them on their journey.

OSHUN: Awareness is where it begins. From that point you begin to see your oppression, the ways your reality is constructed by others. As a Black woman you realize the suffocating binds of race, class, and gender and how this triple bind affects your lived existence (Beale, 1995; King, 1992).

ROCHELLE: This is difficult and even worrisome because as I perceive myself, as I understand and analyze self, I see the whole of me and I see the parts. According to Dill (1994), "we must examine on an analytical level the ways in which the structures of class, race, and gender intersect in any woman's or group of women's lives in order to grasp the concrete set of social relations that influence their behavior" (p. 47). I am trying to understand the influence race, class, and gender have on the ways these women make meaning of their life, construct how they know what they know.

OSHUN: And?

ROCHELLE: An important part of who they are and how they reach understanding is framed within their identity as Black women. For instance, when I asked Grace her purpose she replied although she was still searching for her purpose, she knew that an integral part of it was connected with being a Black woman. Likewise, Veronica, when explaining her identity concept map, stated that she had placed on the borders the word African American woman, not because that was marginal to her life but because it was who she was and what defined everything else. Throughout the conversation, being a Black woman was a framing perspective for the women and a conscious piece of their self. As we each analyzed our life we did so from the social, historical, and cultural landscape of our Black womanism.

OSHUN: I noticed that one of the major points of interest was all of the women had varying degrees of a Black female consciousness. Grace has moved into accepting both parts of her being—her race and her gender—as one whole, which is different from when you interviewed her last year. At that point Grace viewed them as two separate entities and even had difficulty using Black woman as a self-descriptor in a sentence. Last year when you asked her about being a Black woman she stated,

> There is a definite difference. . . . The outside image I don't know because we are at the bottom and we do so much and we are so strong and we carry so much and we go through so much that I don't understand the stereotypes—the attitude thing—I don't understand how we don't get any credit for anything. It is very hard and I think that is why I made them separate, because how can I be this person, me knowing myself, all the things I think I am and then there is this image. But that's not me but that's me, I am a Black woman but that image isn't me. I think that's why I separate them and I think that's why a lot of people do. (Interview 4/01/98)

ROCHELLE: As a teacher it is exciting to see the transformation and growth in how Grace defines herself. In a paper she wrote for me one year later she started it with,

I am a strong Black Woman. I am a strong Black Woman. I am a strong Black woman. [3 x 4 ur mind]. I say it first because I am. I say it again to make sure you hear me, to make sure you listen and not tune out as you did the first time. I say it a third time so you can feel me. I say it because I am. (4/10/99)

The ability to say I am, to define self for self, and not to fall into the definition of others is paramount to survival (Hale-Benson, 1986; Collins, 1991; hooks, 1981). The movement in Grace's consciousness from denial to acceptance and love in her Black femaleness grows out of her spiritualness and her commitment to critically accept knowledge. hooks teaches us that

> Living a life with spirit, a life where our habits of being enable us to hear our inner voices, to comprehend reality with both our hearts and our minds, puts us in touch with divine essence. Practicing the art of loving is one way we sustain contact with our "higher self." (1993, p. 185)

OSHUN: Spirituality was vital to all of the women. Spirituality is essential to life, as I feel it. "It is a living, growing thing which has spread forth across the world and through the nations, affecting everything that it touches" (Hayes, 1995, p. 56). A connection with God was an influential component of how they understood their lives, as well as how they understood and accepted a commitment to humanity outside of self. In their descriptions, spirituality, Christianity, child of God were mentioned. Even the women who said they were searching for what it meant to lead a life as a Christian expressed belief in the importance of finding the answer.

ROCHELLE: The importance of family was another commonality amongst all of the women, especially their relationships with their mothers. Respecting, admiring and learning from the wisdom of mothers and othermothers is a reality in the Black tradition (Hayes, 1995; hooks, 1993). These young women admired their mothers and at the same time they realized the faults their mothers possessed by internalizing the stereotypes placed on them as Black women. The burden of always having to be strong, taking care of everything and everybody. They knew that such a burden was too heavy for anyone to carry. The women were determined to change that cycle by becoming more aware than their mothers were.

OSHUN: Awareness led them to a health of spirit and soul. It is awareness, which allows the women to move further into their Black consciousness. By Black consciousness I mean not only accepting being Black women but the political struggle that comes with it. A Black consciousness means accepting the responsibility for your community by working for your community, whether it be mentoring, teaching, or helping to build an economic infrastructure in the Black community. A Black consciousness means teaching other Black people. It means social responsibility. It means being able to think and act critically. It means being aware of the social, political, and historical forms of oppression.

It means being aware of the present forms of oppression. It means knowing the face of the enemy and knowing the bullet needed to kill.

ROCHELLE: Rather than experiencing life as a chess piece in a game played by someone else, the women of sista dialogue were finding ways to be in charge of self. Self-reflection provided the women with a way into their inner self. Self-reflection involved constantly questioning the world and their placement in it. As various personal situations were discussed, the women attempted to gain an understanding from both a personal and a theoretical view by questioning why they were able to effectively critically deconstruct the context.

Their ability to critically deconstruct was exciting and I needed a style that would highlight their discourse. I had an extremely difficult time deciding what was most important to include. Writing a "typical" analysis chapter was too confining. I tried and I could not make the reader feel the words and thoughts of the women by simply taking chunks out here and there. Everything was part of the whole six hours and I struggled with doing justice to the time these women spent in my home, trying to give me what they knew I needed. Providing removed slices of the conversation followed by my analysis would not allow the holistic view of the women which is so important in my research. Instead, what I present to you in "Sista to Sista to Sista: A Story in Three Acts" are bits and pieces of our dialogue.

Reflection
SILENCE

I do not weep at the world / I am too busy sharpening my oyster knife
—Zora Neale Hurston

"I don't love you anymore," he said while removing the angel from the top of the now-dead Christmas tree. "Our marriage is wrong. I still love her. I need to leave you. Tonight."

He continued talking; sitting perched like a vulture on top of the ladder, twirling the angel between his palms. She kneeled on the floor beneath him in a sea of empty ornament boxes, lights, garland, and candy canes. All the paraphernalia of Christmas. Their New Year's Eve ritual had always been for him to remove and her to repack the Christmas ornaments. She insisted that a tree left standing after midnight on New Year's Eve would leave the door open for the bad of the old year to be ushered into the new. She also fixed black-eyed peas for New Year's dinner and buried a dollar every New Year's Eve only to retrieve it at dawn. Her mother had told her these traditions would bring luck. She loved traditions and rituals. It was as if they connected the past and the present. She had practiced these as a child and as a woman they became part of her home.

She realized that although he was still talking she had stopped listening. His words were not about her. It was impossible to stop loving a person in just one day. Love wasn't a faucet that runs hot and cold with the turn of the spigot. He must have had too much Christmas eggnog. She laughed, maybe to herself, maybe out loud. She wasn't sure. She tried to listen to what he was now saying but the only word she could hear was divorce. It fell from his lips, floated down to where she sat and simply hovered above her head. She sat, with her eyes closed, tight, but her mind's eye could still see that "word." Like a flashing neon sign the "word" was illuminated in her head. Quickly she opened her eyes and the "word" crashed into her, shattering her insides like so many tiny fragments of glass. So as not to hear anymore she filled her mind with random thoughts. . .

it's getting late i have to take the tree down badluck badluck return gifts if only my feet weren't so large i could keep the shoes cut the toes they would be perfect manicure haircut mother i must call

. . . that made no sense when viewed as a whole. The sense was between, underneath and around each word.

He still talked. To her, to himself, it did not matter. "Shut Up!" she thought. "I don't want your words, keep them, choke on them, let them smother you as they are smothering me." Of course this she said to herself, to him she said nothing.

She sat afraid to move, staring at the ornament she still clutched in her hand. She could not feel herself breathing, inhaling or exhaling. NUMB. Her legs were stiff but she dare not shift her body to a more comfortable position. If she moved even a fraction, if she allowed her mind to say that her body was real then the situation would become real.

She felt him leave the room. She heard noise coming from the bedroom. Sounds of packing. Drawers opening and closing. Rattle of wire hangers. The grating sound of the zipper being closed on the suitcase. Her hearing was keen; the sounds were so loud it was as if they were inside her head. She remained still, not saying anything, not crying, trying her best not to even feel. The last sound she heard was the closing of the front door.

He did not say good-bye.

Several times he came back only to leave again. She never talked about how she felt. Not to him, her family, her friends, not to herself. She had learned to keep it all locked inside. When she did venture to tell someone how she felt, the advice was "Be strong. Grin and bear it. You are better off without him." So she remained silent.

She did not know how to vocalize what she felt so she went inside herself. She built a wall, brick by brick, for protection against hurt. She started a diary, wrote pages of nothing. She went to sad movies so not to cry alone. Her sorrow was her own, not to be shared.

She was lonely.

The days passed. The tears flowed. She secluded herself in what was once their home. Not wanting to see people. What could they do or say to make the pain go away? Nothing. Did she even want the pain to leave. It was in a way comforting. It was the only thing that let her know she still had some semblance of life or living. It, the pain, was the blanket that kept her warm at night. As long as the pain was there she did not have to wake up alone.

As secluded as she tried to keep herself, she could never run from her thoughts. They stayed with her. Bumping against the corners of her mind. Questions, recriminations, musings, questions. But never the answers she needed.

One morning, not long after he left for the last time, she woke with her blanket of pain. It was so heavy, it weighed her down. Even trying to get out of bed required more energy, more exertion then she was capable of. How had it happened? When did her "self" become his? Did she ever have a real "self" or had it always been tied into that of others? When you define your existence based on the ideals of others, you give them power. More power over you than you have over yourself. When you do not or cannot define yourself then who do you become? A shell, someone who is weak, can be manipulated, dies a slow death daily. You are never what you were the day before because your existence was fleeting, never tied to reality.

She began to cry hot, mean tears as the blanket of pain got heavier. Each memory added weight to what was already too heavy to bear. The little girl whom she was became the woman whom she is. The pain, the lack of identity that began to develop as a child came to fruition as an adult. She tried to turn over, move herself into a different position and caught sight of her tear-stained face in the mirror. It was as if she was looking at someone else. A stranger. Even though she could feel and taste the tears that flowed freely the woman in the mirror with the tear-streaked face was a stranger. A fool. She stared at that image hoping that if she looked deep enough she could determine the exact moment when she became invisible. When she stopped believing in her dreams. Became afraid of dreaming.

She had dreamed little girl dreams. She had dreamed the dreams of a woman. The empty place could be filled; the incomplete place could be made whole. So she had married and prayed her identity could be given to her through love. He told her he did not love her. He told her he did not want her. He told her not to dream the dreams of fools so she woke up.

How many dreams had died when she woke up. How many hopes had died when she stopped dreaming. What could have been born in her if others, people whose names or faces she no longer remembered, had said instead to dream the dreams of fools and make those dreams reality. What would have been different in her life if she had said yes to possibilities? What would have been different if as child and then as a woman she had found her voice and used it to shout.

Her tears, which had been angry and full of self-pity, flowed freely. She cried for the lost child she was, she cried for all the lost Black girls who did not know who they were, who defined themselves in relation to and comparison with social constructions based on nothingness and hate. Every tear became a tear for their lost dreams. Every hurt became a hurt for the lost lives of innocent children. Children whose only crime was being born a woman and Black.

At last the tears would no longer come. The pain remained. There still existed within her an emptiness. Somehow though it was different. She realized that she had allowed society and others, with their rules to condition her to remain silent, be a victim. She had never been taught the rules of the game; therefore she was always at a disadvantage when playing. Never knowing herself, never trusting in herself made it so easy for others to take away what little she had. Her hurt was not really caused by others but the control she allowed them to have over her. Slowly she lifted the blanket that had become part of her. Wiping the tears from her face she sat up. Tentatively at first and then with more assurance than she had felt in a lifetime she stood. She knew that although it would be difficult, with work she could redefine who she was, be in control of her own destiny. She had the power to make her life the way she wanted it to be. She had the power to define who she was and who she wanted to become. She had the right and the obligation to survive.

> My divorce, although painful, provided me with a new level of understanding and compassion, one that I infuse throughout my pedagogy. As I attempted to understand the hurt and confusion in my life at the time I came to value the interconnected nature of existence. How the pieces of my past and the pieces of the past of those who inhabited the same space as I constantly constructed a changing reality in my present. I needed to theorize away the pain and see my way into a spiritual healing. Once I began to heal I could place my divorce, its causes, and my reactions within a contextualized life. My past became my present and my future inextricably tied together making me whole.

four

Sista to Sista to Sista:
A Story in Three Acts

The story takes place in Rochelle's apartment. All scenes are acted out in her small living room. A neighbor brings over a low-fat banana cake for the group and hurriedly departs with a wish of good luck. The aroma of cooking chili and lavender-scented candles greet the senses upon entering the room. The mood is tense, waiting for what is to come. Stephanie is busy setting up two cameras, each on opposite sides of the room. Strategically placed on the desk and coffee table are small tape recorders. Rochelle paces, then checks the recorders for the hundredth time. The women begin to arrive.

Story One:
The Rage Within: Anger and Black Women

> It is not the anger of other women that will destroy us but our refusals to stand still, to listen to its rhythms, to learn within it, to move beyond the manner of presentation to the substance, to tap that anger as an important source of empowerment. (Lorde, 1996b, p. 130)

VERONICA: Another problem is with the professors. I've come across some professors this semester and I feel like I'm fighting every day in these classes and these are professors that have these issues while it's not blatantly ignorant, it's just, they'll say things off their faces and have these goofy smiles and they're like. . . At moments I have even no idea where to begin to explain to this person, why what they said was ignorant or why what they said was wrong. It's like well, what battle should I choose? How is this going to affect my grade? I've been accused of being the chick with the attitude. "Oh God, you have such a chip on your shoulder" and I'm thinking, You may have heard me raise my voice you know, I'm kind of calm here, I'm trying to explain some things to you, and I'm still getting this. And then me being sensitive and then it's like now I'm the chick with the chip on her shoulder and would you say this to me if I was not Black. . .

Education, the embodiment of "manifest destiny." Throughout the discussion the ways education works to hide racism and the inability of White teachers and White students to deal with or even acknowledge its existence was a point of contention with the women. King (1994b) asserts that "Dysconscious racism is a form of racism that tacitly accepts dominant White norms and privileges" and "is an uncritical habit of mind (including perceptions, attitudes, and beliefs) that justify inequality and exploitation by accepting the existing order of things as given." (p. 338)

And the thing for me, like you said that you have kind of talked about race and difference since you were younger. My childhood was so filled with other stuff that I didn't really get sensitive about being a Black female or anything until maybe my senior year in high school because there was so much other chaos going on in my house. You know, I guess those dysfunctional houses that you see on TV were mine. And so it was so much other stuff that I was fighting through and just being angry in general at my situation. Until that smoothed out, which I must have been about fifteen when it smoothed out, I was able to go, "Oh, well now there's problems, there's other situations, there's other things to fight for" and then it hit me gradually and it was sometimes I was like, I remember referring to myself as not being, you know, when people would give a speech for this or talk about that, I was like I don't know nothing about that stuff. I'm not Afrocentric. I used to say all kinds of stupid stuff out of my mouth. You know, I'm not writing no speech for blank. Where, what? You know, I'm Black, I'm cool, it's OK.

We ask what happens to a person's being when they grow up without a sense of self? Growing up, Veronica and many of her friends were not concerned with issues of race, but instead with issues of survival. Being Black was a norm, it was what she was. Being poor was a norm, it was her reality. Although Veronica attended an all-Black public elementary school she was not provided with a foundation on which to build a Black consciousness at a young age. Establishing a cultural and racial identity is critical for African American children. Murrell (1997) asserts that "A critical literacy for all children must work toward promoting the sensibilities, skills, and knowledge necessary for critically interpreting experiences and resolving "dilemmas of belonging' as children move in and out of different cultural scenes between home and school." (p. 42)

VERONICA: I never really got involved until I was confronted with it, and mainly here. Here was the main place, I must say, I've been confronted with stuff to the point that I am now getting pissed and I think that's why I'm so frustrated because it's all smacking me in the face, like every day, like constantly. Opposed to dealing with it growing up, it wasn't the main thing. I wasn't really around White people that much and if I was it was my teacher in an inner-city school and she dealt with all Black kids or when I finally did go to a big school, the Black kids was over here and the White kids was here, I didn't have a problem with it, my neighborhood was all Black, my schools were all

Black before, so that's kind of the way things were supposed to be. I didn't really think about it until I got here, maybe until I started college when I was in New York I had some things there too, but mainly here. I guess that's my biggest frustration, these professors, because if I can't even get it in their heads, how am I gonna possibly converse with anybody on that level in my class?

> *The way others perceive Black women troubles the interactions these Black women have with professors, students, friends, etc. All of the women stated that being at State, a predominantly White environment which was also hostile, forced them to think about and deal with their Blackness. Prior to State most had never experienced an African American course and therefore not been confronted with the historical reality of the Black existence. Once they began to learn Black history, coupled with the hostility of the environment, their new level of awareness brought anger.*

CAROLE: And they're supposed to be educated.

VERONICA: But I think when they're from towns from out here, you know, how educated can they possibly be, and that's why I've tried not to get angry with them, because it's like, "You don't know, you're like a little kid that just are saying what you seen on TV or you're saying what somebody else said to you." But they're like naive children at forty-something years of age or fifty-something years of age or older saying just crazy stuff out of their mouths, and so I think that's why I'm so. . .

> *Although these women understand the ignorance involved in racist action and thought, they are still affected. Their frustration lay in the knowledge that if at their young age and level of education they understood constructions of the other, why could not the older and supposedly more educated do so as well.*

CHINA: It depends, also, the type of class. There are so many different grades of just White people. You can get some ones that are trying to be more outspoken, but my whole thing is, as I listen to White people say certain things, I almost can see their ignorance. . . . You almost sort of, not necessarily understand them, but like when that one White girl was like, "well if everybody just. . .and we all have puppies. . .and everybody's happy," like I can almost see her and understand her point of view because she's coming from this White girl that never had to deal with any issues. I'm not excusing their ignorance, but I can almost understand it because I'm looking like, well, shoot, if I was White, I wouldn't really care about y'all. It would only be on some. . . I can almost see it.

ROCHELLE: What makes a White person get outside their privilege and understand where somebody else is from?

VERONICA: They seem almost desperate to stay in that. Like, "Oh, please, can we just get along?" No more difference, if we could just all be the same! It's a desperate level.

CHINA: That's the thing. They stripped. . . they're the ones that stripped everybody, so they're still. . . looking like, "What's the problem?"

CAROLE: But. . . I find that easier to fight in the fact that you know what you're confronting. Because there are some people, like White people on this campus that are, I don't know if I would call them a racist, but they don't, they themselves don't even know their views and what they feel about certain things, so you're confronting something that you don't know, you're going into like a dark room.

JENNIFER: And that's what causes me to lose sleep. I try to be optimistic. I came in here. I know I was going into a predominantly White setting, and I get in here and I'm teaching these kids and I'm like, all right, I'm showing them they gotta have a world view. . . Yeah, right, and what scares me is that the syrupy, "Everything's okay here in…, and nothing happens," are teaching our students and that's why they're not able to deal with race.

CAROLE: But the thing is what's even scarier, is that I'm sitting next to those, and they're learning this from State,* and I'm thinking to myself, "I do not want my students, my kids, when I have kids, in their classroom." And they're going to be touching so many lives. I respect all professions, but I think teaching is such a dangerous job and people don't even realize it, you know? We touch so many lives.

The inability of White people in the education system, whether at State or in the public school system, to deal with difference was a source of great anger for the women.

JENNIFER: Yeah, and then what you do. . . which is gonna get me in trouble now, but I'll bring in what I'm teaching. . . and the teachers will be like "but, that's not in the curriculum!"

STACY: If you get down about it, just think, what if you weren't there to teach little kids this.

VERONICA: I totally understand that. I keep a butterfly in my stomach. What did I say today? Get my self-esteem on this project and I know I deserve a B or an A. You know, it's just constantly, every class I go to it's like now you gotta bad. . . "What did I say? Did I say that right? Did my voice escalate?" Cause sometimes, I don't even know. Sometimes it starts low, like you just said, it starts, "I don't wanna come at you and I want to ask you something concerning blah, blah, blah," coming to you very diplomatically. And then he goes, "Well you have a heavy chip on your shoulder." I'm like, "What?" I'm like somebody take me out of here please. I'm about to jump over him.

According to Claude Steele (1992), Black children are devalued in the school setting and that experience is doubled because it applies to Blacks in a way that it does not apply to

---

* The title "State" refers to the university where the study took place.

Whites. For example, all students risk devaluation for a failed test, but Black students fear that the failed test (or any other error) will simply confirm the broader racial inferiority of which they are suspected. Throughout schooling, Blacks have the extra fear that others will see their "full humanity fall with a poor answer or a mistaken stroke of the pen" (Jordan-Irvine, 1990, p.74). The students have the burden of constantly having to prove themselves. Furthermore, with each new class and level of schooling the acceptance must be won again. The struggle for Black students to gain acceptance is continuous throughout their schooling. They learn that if acceptance is won, it will be hard-won.

CAROLE: Can I ask some questions? I want to tie it back to African American women for Rochelle's book and since we all, China is the new person here, I want to ask her a question. I've wondered this in class. Earlier we were talking about how we get upset with classes, especially when we're in a White class, like when we're the only Black person and we feel that it's our responsibility to educate and whether or not that is our responsibility and over how we go about it. Speaking to the point, you are a very loud person, you express your feelings, you do not let anybody put you down. And so I was always wondering how do you think people perceive you and how do you know people perceive you when you speak out in classes? How do people react to you? White people in your classes and outside of class?

CHINA: That's a perfect question for the simple fact—it actually happened in class, it was, when was this? Wednesday? OK, it was like Wednesday, in my Comp 404 class, which is Mass Communications Research. My teacher's this little Jewish woman. . . I don't know if she feels like it's her responsibility, but every example that she uses in class, like OK, not every example, but maybe like twice a week, she always wants to use an example with Blacks, so it's kind of like, umm, now mind you, it's a research question, so, "How are African-Americans stereotypes perpetuated in the media?"

STEPHANIE: I think all 404 teachers do that, 'cause my teacher. . .

VERONICA: I think all teachers, period, do that in any Com courses, I think.

CHINA: Why all of a sudden, OK, . . . this happened on Wednesday because Tuesday was the whole thing with Tim and I'm just in this whole thing, I'm not holding my tongue any more. So in class, the class was broken up in two parts. The beginning. . . certain group members have an article to read. So they read the article, and then they talk about it in class and they have a class discussion. So right away, the only person in my class that's Black, aside from me, is Rhonda. That's it. Me and Rhonda. There's no Asians. There's no nothing but White, rural folk in the class. Just cause there are some cool, down, White folks, you know what I mean? At least a White person with a little spunk, you know? There's no spunk in that class except me and Rhonda.

So they talk about this article. Oh, OK, I flipped later in class. The article was about how. . . the way blacks are portrayed in the media affect people's prejudice towards them, was the idea of it. So, you know, I was just kind of calm. I basically joined some work from another class, so I was kind of there, but like, let me have to get through this, it's a two-hour class. So the class, whatever, we talking about this. A couple people made comments and to start addressing the question, automatically, as soon as, of course, the question comes out about African Americans, you know, everybody kind of looks, you know everybody sort of looks at you and then they don't look at you. . . . At least some teachers kind of try to not really look at you, but she sort of looks at you like almost, "What's your opinion?" That type of feel, but anyway, so everybody discussed it. I didn't even say anything. I think Rhonda made a comment and that was it. I didn't feel anything came up that I needed to really say because. . . I automatically feel as soon as I say something, I'm being pegged like, you know what I mean? So I'm trying to almost curb myself so that when I do make a comment, it is at least a comment that has some type of weight to it almost, if you will. Like I don't start, like I don't nitpick. Cause it's almost kind of easier, especially going through a class with Rochelle and you start to begin to understand and see things, you almost want to say, "No, no, that's not right!" you almost want to correct everybody. So I didn't go through that. Then that was the first segment of the class.

> When a minority student is put on the spot in class and asked to speak for their entire race, the teacher is practicing dysconscious racism. In this case the teacher was creating a monolithic view of Blackness by placing China's experience of being Black as the Black experience. She did not see the complexities of Blackness or the intersection of race/class/gender on specific realities of specific Black people. Worse this teacher did not want to see—it was easier (perhaps safer) to hold onto her narrow view of the other.

The second segment, she pops on the overhead and the question, and this is when the question was, okay take a breath, basically the idea of the research question was, "If Whites learn more about African Americans' history, will there be a lessening in prejudice?" was the idea. But I can't quite remember the wording of it, but the wording of it started to make me feel hot because it was almost like, I felt, from my point of view, from where I was sitting, it looked like, "Well, if White people learn about Black people's culture, then they'll be OK." Like you know what I mean? Then prejudice will help to be eliminated if they learn more about us. My attitude is, you know? Who the fuck are you? Why does there have to be the fact that if you learn more about us, then we're OK? Or if you read up your history and see, oh they're not so bad—that was the whole tone of it. If they educate themselves, then they'll see that we're not that bad.

So, as she continues to talk on and on, I raised my hand and I said, "You know, I was just wondering why for the last couple of weeks, just about every other example that you use deals with Black and White race issues." I said, "I feel as though there are so many other races, nationalities, ethnicities, other people that you can use. . . ." I started saying Cubans and Dominicans and Puerto Ricans and Chinese and Japanese. I started going on like that and ending up that "there are so many other cultures that embody the 'American society' that you can use as examples, I'm just curious as to why you always want to use Black and White"? And her face went red like that Coca-Cola can. Do you all hear me? Like she was "Well, I mean, these are the examples that I'm giving that's from the books that we use."

"I would just hope that professors would use more discretion in the fact that there's only two minorities in this entire class, and when I say minorities, there's nothing else in here, but White folk." And then that's when I started feeling myself, I was like, China breath down, 'cause I started to say White folks and something about saying White folks makes me want to riot. White folks. I didn't say White people. I didn't say Caucasian. I said White folks. I said, "There's nothing but White folks in here." And she's like, "Well," and then, of course, a (White) girl raised her hand. . . She raised her hand, "Well, I can understand what you're saying, but like, I mean, it really doesn't have to always be about race because I don't really see what's wrong with the example really, it's just education. If White people like myself were to educate ourselves, then race relations would be so much better in this world and everything would be so much better, so really, the example is just to try to make things better." I just looked at her, and then this White guy raised his hand. "Well, I can see what she's saying." Now all of a sudden, automatically, SHE, so I disappeared into, like, I made my point, but now the White folks have come out to discuss it, so automatically, it's she. "Well, I understand where she's coming from. . . ." So then the discussion almost became everybody else but me. And I had raised the point. You feel that. What was his point? I don't even remember because by this point I was so mad and I felt so mad and helpless. I felt like I needed more Black people, like I needed Miss Rochelle. I needed somebody else there to almost argue for me because I almost felt out of my league, like I had stepped beyond what I could almost argue.

ROCHELLE: Or what you could articulate.

CHINA: Exactly, so it was almost like, whoa, but that's not what I was saying, you know what I mean? And then I almost felt like, and then almost the tone basically was like, "Why do they keep complaining?" Like "Get over it." It was almost like a get over it. So then everybody is just kind of like. . . and I said, "Well," and that's when I just brought it from here to almost end the discussion because I was like, "Basically what SHE is saying is that SHE feels offended because of the simple fact that every example or every example used in this class deals with race, Black and White. There's other issues and there's other topics. . ." and she was like, "Well, I don't see why it's so bad, maybe". . . and I was just like, "You know what? You really don't get it, but actually, I don't expect you to. I just want you to understand that I feel uncomfortable as a Black woman."

The need to reassert, reclaim, redefine the self in discourse was evident for all of the women. They were intent on naming their reality. Throughout the dialogue it was always clear that in classroom situations where these women were effectively being forced into an uncomfortable position they were not afraid to speak up. Often they were more vocal in a classroom situation than in their personal relationships with family and friends.

ROCHELLE: Do you think it's part of, like earlier we were talking about choosing your battles and figuring out which battle is worthwhile?

VERONICA: What I find, and I really thank you for letting me be here, because I now know that I am not by myself. I felt so alone. That's why I was losing sleep and all kinds of stuff, because if I'm in a class, and like you said, it's you and maybe one other Black person in the class, and while the other Black person might be nodding their head and not saying a word, and like you said, you get so filled up and you get so hot. I felt hot.

Veronica thanked me several times throughout the six hours for including her in the group. She repeatedly talked about feeling alone in her struggle and in her anger and feeling somehow vindicated knowing that the other women were experiencing the same or similar feelings as she.

CAROLE: I think one of the things we can do is, as we said earlier, is pick our battles and speak up. The thing is. . .

VERONICA: I was never so angry as when I took your class and was reading. . . I was like, "Oh!" Even our bodies—Men are doing it to us.

ROCHELLE: That's why they call it. . . what do we do?

CAROLE: But you know what? I think not only is the line what do we do? But how we go about it? A lot of us said that we're creative in our descriptions. There are so many ways of confronting people who are ignorant. You don't always have to be a preacher or you don't always have to be the angry, Black woman. Personally, I've had instances where someone will say something and I'll go along with it and I'll make fun of it to the point where they realize what they're saying, but it's through humor. There's other ways about doing it and I think that's something that we can also keep in mind.

Every battle deserves, and must have its own, distinct strategy for victory.

CHINA: . . .Yes, we're all Black women or all Black females, but we all such distinct different personalities, so maybe that's the way for you to handle it and that's wonderful because you know at times I do wish I didn't feel that way. I do almost wish I could bring it down, but. . .maybe a factor of maturity almost, because I guess as you get older, you almost begin to. . . but to me almost, it's like when you become mature, you almost begin to lose that light. People saying, "Oh, well you need to be more mature." If one more person tells me to watch myself and think before I speak. . . I've been hearing it since I've been this big, plus I'm an only child, so I'm always in trouble. But it's the fact that there comes a point when I feel like I'll never be this young and this vocal and this excited and this into and this passionate about such a cause. That I almost feel like, so what? Dammit, if I have an outburst or if I feel like I need to express this passion, then I'm gonna do that. If people have a problem with it, well then they have a problem with it. They can speak back. There's a way I can articulate myself. There's a way I can go about things, but I can't stay silent.

CAROLE: For me, as a person who is more on the quieter side, I respect that because I'm not like that. I'm not the person who's going to be. . . I will speak and I am always the one who's the only minority in my class, and I'm the person who always. . . I do talk in my class. I do bring up the race issue. I do it whatever happens and I do correct people. I go about it a different way than you do. When I see people like you who go about it, I respect that and I would help you out in the class, but I would not be as, like I don't know what the word is I'm looking for, never mind.

ROCHELLE: Aggressive. Maybe assertive.

CAROLE: . . . as assertive as you are. You know?

CHINA: And it's this class, I'm telling y'all. Like you said you were never really angry. Of course, I would always be like, I might have still said something, but I guess also that's why, Carole you made the point where you began to just also. . .

CAROLE: Open your eyes.

CHINA: . . . because as soon as I began to become educated and I could articulate and began to really put pieces together. Well, wait a minute. Through your class, I can almost say, wait, something's not right and now I can almost say why it's not right. Or I can at least, through your class. . .

CAROLE: Justify your feelings. Know why you feel a certain way.

Knowledge and anger is a dangerous combination. The more knowledge you possess, the more you are able to name your oppression, the angrier you become.

CHINA: Everything is starting to come together. I'm seeing the whole picture and that is where I think the anger is. . .I'm really like, everything is coming into focus and as I begin to get clearer and clearer, I get more and more disturbed.

GRACE: I think, cause I'm sitting here and I know, I'm just angry. I get angry. Angry, angry, angry. I don't think that I, even in my daily life, I don't express my anger. I hold it in until I snap. I know when I was in Rochelle's *Racism and Sexism* class, I was going crazy. The people were driving me insane.

I was like, "Rochelle, I don't understand it. People are making me sick. I'm not talking because. . ." They were just. . . I loved the class.

ROCHELLE: One time in particular I remember why you got angry and it was really interesting because everybody in class was being, we had twenty students, six African-American, the rest White. Three Black women, and three Black men. Everybody was talking politically correct. Grace got mad in her log that night, I remember she was like, "I'm not gonna talk about the reading. I'm gonna talk about the class. Everybody is saying that they're not racist. They're not this, they're not that." I remember she had this paragraph, cause it actually ended up in one of my papers. She's like; "I know that when I walk down the street with John, people look at me funny. I know that I was scared when my boyfriend would drive back home late at night. I know this, I know that." And then she ended with, "I know that I know that I know." She was trying her damnedest not to doubt what she knew to be true.

> When White people refused to acknowledge issues of race all of the women said that for a moment it made them doubt if what they felt and knew was real. I say for a moment because the women were grounded in their knowledge and as Grace wrote in her log, "I Know That I Know."

GRACE: Yeah, they make you, a lot of it, I remember the one particular point we were talking. . . trying to incite conflict and try to get us to talk more, to interact because the class was this way. . . . They were talking about interracial couples. So they would ask the Black females, "How do you feel about whatever?" They would ask the Black males, "How do you feel about whatever?" We were talking. Then they asked White males and we had a couple, we had more than a couple White males.

ROCHELLE: About four or five.

GRACE: Yeah, so, "How do you feel when a White girl is walking down the street with a Black man?" "No problem." Oh! The White girl, "How do you feel when a Black girl is with a White man, or vice versa?" "No problem. If they in love, you know, whatever." That's when I flipped. Then it got to the point, the girls, everybody White was looking at us, and what's her name? Chante?

ROCHELLE: Chante. Chantelle, I think it was.

GRACE: No, Sharmelle. It was me and her and we're sitting there, like we know you're lying. You're just lying. Just come out. Then it was to the point, "Well do you want us to be racist. You want us to feel this way. Why do you want us to feel this way?" That's what I mean by the crazy. Then I started to get angry.

> According to King (1994b), when people do not have a critical consciousness it "involves an ethical judgment about the social order"; those involved in dysconscious racism accept the social order uncritically (p. 338). The women in sista dialogue expressed the anger

they felt when others, specifically the White students, refused to think about the problems of racism on a deeper level. As a friend of mine said in a conversation, "If White people were fine with race then why do we have the level of hate that we do?" The women were trying to answer this question.

GRACE: Then it comes even to this class, just the stuff we're talking about, I'm angry. This is personal, but I really, this all goes to the Black, vulnerable and all that, because, about two years ago, I got seriously depressed. DEPRESSED. I was on my couch like this [curled in a fetal position]. I was depressed. Like medication. Like going to the doctor. Not doing anything, family's work, anything. That was my weakness, OK, and I've been dealing with it since. Now that I've shown, and people's like, "What the hell happened?" I was so, everything was supposedly OK, and then all of a sudden, I break down. It was just because I was overwhelmed. I was stressed and I had no outlets. It's as simple as that. Got a lot of shit going on. I had nowhere to feed it to. No one's getting it, you know? I didn't because whatever. So I got depressed, and I'm sitting there, and I felt like a baby. My friends were calling me. My TRUE friend and my mother and other people in my family were calling me all the time and my friend would call me every day, "What are you doing? How are you?" Whatever. My so-called friend, my angel sisters, and we had just crossed after that. . .

So, nobody called me. Nobody wondered. I see them, not after I got better, but after I was able to deal with things, and move on with my life, I had seen them at a party, "Well, where you been?" Well, if you would have called me. . . and that would piss me off. 'Cause here it is, I went through the worst time in my life, y'all don't call me. Same apartment number. Didn't go home. I was up here in this place. Y'all didn't call me. People I had classes with, they didn't care that I had dropped out the whole semester. Do you know what I mean? That's why, bullshit. That's what I don't get. And that's why I don't. . . you call me the other day, talking about, "Are you going out?"

Although Grace believed her depression showed weakness by allowing herself the freedom to "breakdown" she actually showed strength. With all of her insights into self she nevertheless internalizes society's definitions of strength.

GRACE: I used to be out there. I used to be all for community. I used to be all for this place and about community; doing everything, and I told you that. But where's the give and take in that situation?
CHINA: Girl, I'm starting, I'm just saying that I'm beginning to think of issues I've dealt with even just in the last two weeks. Just with the haters. And the people, I can see in their eyes the fact that they don't have my best interests at heart. My mother's always taught me to look in eyes and you can see everything. Just the fact that I can look in eyes and see people that don't have my best interests at heart. My own people. My own female sisters. Like my

own sisterhood. I have this whole passion thing for them, but I'm not getting that back. I can see how I'm slowly ostracizing myself out of that social circle. I'm also beginning to see. . .

Black folk culture says to look in the eyes and see the soul of a person. The women are beginning to see what was hidden.

VERONICA: Girl, I did that before I got here.

CHINA: I'm beginning to come into my own awareness. I'm beginning to see the fakeness. I'm starting to see cracks in the picture. Everything isn't looking as it used to look. It's not always about this. It's so much depth to different issues that people just want to stay up here on the surface. Nobody wants to dig with me.

The conversation switches to a confrontation China had in class with a Black male student.

ROCHELLE: Let me start it and then, China, you take it. We were talking about stereotypes. China mentioned something about token, Will Smith being a token and then Tim, the guy China got into the argument with. . .

VERONICA: Is he White?

ROCHELLE: He's Black.

CHINA: For the record, all he dates is White women. That's all he dates. So just between us and for the film or whatever, him and me had talked for like a minute, like when I first transferred up here, I think I was too much for him.

To China, and the other women, there was consensus that Tim dating only White women was indicative of his larger rejection of Black womanhood. Interestingly, Tim called me often during the class and expressed that my class and I had helped him reach a new level of maturity. Could it be that I represented a mother figure and therefore not a Black woman so I was easier to accept?

CHINA: Rochelle, he only dates White women, so therefore when he disrespected me, I took it up on a whole other level, knowing that. Like he does not respect us.

ROCHELLE: So, China said Will Smith was just a token. Tim stepped in and said that a token was somebody, Tim was looking at token in the wrong way. He was looking at token like a sambo-stereotype. He was just. . .

CHINA: He was wrong.

ROCHELLE: He was disagreeing with China. So then I came in and I said, no, China is right. Will Smith is a token. A token is when they only let one or a few come out. Like we have Will Smith as a serious actor. We only have Denzel as a sex symbol. . . you have many sex symbols for White males. . . so then Tim's like, "Oh, okay, I understand what you're saying." Then China said, "That's the same thing I said."

CHINA: Like, thank you Miss Rochelle. I always have a mouth in class and normally people are just like, yeah, one of those.

ROCHELLE: But when China said that, then Tim. . .

VERONICA: What did he say? What did he say to you?

CHINA: Y'all just trying to bring me there.

VERONICA: What did you say?

CHINA: Trying to bring me back to that. I'm about to get off the moment. Grab my coat and leave, 'cause I'm about to feel that moment again. . . . He had his hand up, so he was like, "I've got my hand up" or something like that, whatever, I was like whatever because for the last three or four weeks, Tim has been having certain issues I guess that he's dealing with me. I don't know what's going on. I don't speak to him outside of class. Nothing.

> China was reading beyond what was being said to WHAT was being said. There is the misnomer that the oppressed are not aware of there own oppression and therefore cannot speak for themselves. China was not blinded by ideology or some unseen outside force that defined and controlled. Instead, she was able to dismantle the taken-for-granted "truths" because she understood the "constructed reality" in which she exists (Green, 1994).

VERONICA: What did he say?

CHINA: It wasn't. . .

VERONICA: What did he say?

CHINA: To the point, I just wanted to set up the fact that he's constantly just the most tiniest, biting comments constantly. When I was talking to Carla, he's like, "I got my hand up." I was like. . . "Yeah, but wait a minute" and I was getting back to Carla's point. He's sitting about four, three seats in front of me. . .

GRACE: He wasn't that far, you could have yanked him.

CHINA: I should have. . . Automatically, where he's sitting, is almost already on a dismissal because he's in front of me, okay, just to set up that feel. I was like, "Yeah, but Carla. . ." and he was like, "Shut the fuck up, China." But just "Shut the fuck up, China" like. . .

ROCHELLE: Like, dismissal.

CHINA: Yes. Dismissal. The hand, too, it was just "shut the fuck up China" anyway, my point was. . . I was like steaming.

VERONICA: He got vibes. Like what you gonna do?

CHINA: My thing is that first, this isn't the first time so it's not like say he got a little too familiar too soon, and I can almost be like, "fuck you" and leave it there. This has been continual where nobody else has seen it because the class is constantly, people say comments back and forth. . .

GRACE: And people always do this to China, she had to say something. Flipped is not the word. China stood up.

CHINA: . . . It was offensive 'cause he cursed. . . "Is there something you need to say to me Tim? because my thing is, if you want to talk behind your back, if you don't feel, but if you want to whisper something and constantly say something under your breath to me, then lets me know. . . that you have some type of problem with me and something deep-seated, so if we need to get this out in the air, then let's do this, and you need to tell me what the problem is. If you don't have a problem, then you shut the fuck up."

ROCHELLE: And then Tim was still saying something under his breath but China wasn't allowing the dismissal.

CHINA: I wasn't allowing it. I'm through. I'm not letting anybody else dismiss me. I'm empowered. I'm through. I'm not letting anybody else disrespect me. . . I'm not gonna be picked on. I'm not gonna allow everybody to sit up here and shit on me. I'm not gonna allow Tim to open the door for everybody in the class to decide anytime I say something, people dismiss as not important. I deal with that shit every day, White people are always dismissing me. I don't need to go into a class that I love and I feel comfortable with and I thrive to go to and have people dismissing me or making my comments seem almost not as important as the other person. I'm not gonna allow that. Fuck that. Shoot.

> For China there is not a mystification of oppression of self as an object to be controlled and manipulated. As she so succinctly put it, "I'm not letting anybody dismiss me. . . White people are always dismissing me."

GRACE: Come outside.

ROCHELLE: That was really funny though. That was so funny when she said, "We can take it outside."

GRACE: My mouth was on the floor and I love you. . .

ROCHELLE: And then, after China said that. . . there was maybe two minutes left in class, Carla's like, "OK, and on that note."

CHINA: I had to dismiss class that day and I had to apologize to the class the next week and I had to let the class know on a lower level that I apologize first and foremost to Miss Rochelle for disrespecting her class like that 'cause I love her and I wouldn't do that, but I just wanted you as a class to know why I disrupted your education for a moment. That I was very disrespected and offended and this wasn't the first time. I had to nip it in the bud. Maybe the way in which I went about it wasn't the most mature manner. If I had to do it all over again, if I had two minutes to think and breathe about it, maybe I would have spoken to him after class, or maybe I would have gone about it in a more mature manner, but I'm still young. I still have a lot of growing up to do. I still have a lot of growing up to do period. We're all not perfect. And my temper is one thing that's not necessarily under control.

As the teacher I did not have control on that day. Although some would argue I missed a teachable moment, I could not find it. I understood China's rage; her lack of control in the face of what she believed was complete and total disrespect.

VERONICA: I have that kind of temper too. . . Like I'll flip, but then I'll deal with it for a long time.

CHINA: I'll flip in a minute.

GRACE: See, I don't. I guess I keep it in, but when I flip, it's over. It's over. There's no, can I, would you, please, forgive. You're done, end of book, it's over. Don't come back, ever.

CHINA: Miss Rochelle, I love the way you said how, when I talked to her, she called me that night. 'Cause I wanted to say something to you, but I was just so happy to get out of class because I knew a lot of people were like, "Ooh Tim" but I didn't do that for cool points. It's a lot of freshmen and sophomores in the class, so they might think I did it to look like I screamed on him. That was all me. I wasn't, I really could not, I didn't hear you. I didn't see anybody in that class but me and him. I wasn't doing it so that people would think I'm a tough girl. I can be very, I'm tough, I'll kick anybody's ass, but that's just me. I'm tough; I'm a tough girl. But I didn't do it for all that, that was cute in high school, even though I left that there. I was just on that level, and I loved how you told me, don't apologize for my anger or the fact that I felt upset. . .

VERONICA: See that's how I feel. I feel like apologizing for me flipping out. I don't want to, but it's like, how can I come back and be Miss Sane again? 'Cause when I lose it, it's. . . .

ROCHELLE: See, that's why I was telling China that night that I called her, I'm like, "It's OK to be angry. You're not apologizing for being angry at the way you were treated because it was wrong for Tim to say what he said." It was funny when she did come back and apologize to the class; other women in the class agreed with her.

GRACE: They were like, "Oh yeah China" and China was like. . .

ROCHELLE: They're like, "Yeah, you know it was wrong for him to say what he said and to be disrespected by an African American male in a class about African American women." So I told her it's not that you're apologizing for your anger, you're apologizing for the way you expressed it. That's what you're apologizing for, but I don't want you to apologize for being mad, 'cause I think we need to get mad. I think there's some things that we need to get angry about, not everything, 'cause we've already said if we get angry at everything that happens to us, we'd be. . .

Although when the argument occurred everyone was silent, the following class the rest of the women agreed with her anger. Were they silent because they did not see the disrespect until it was pointed out, refusal to back a sister up in need, fear of using their voice, or because the situation was volatile enough and they did not want to add to it? I do not know and did not ask. ". . . to my sisters of Color who like me still tremble their rage as useless and disruptive (the two most popular accusations)—I want to speak about anger, my anger, and what I have learned from my travels through its dominions" (Lorde, 1996b, p. 127).

CHINA: I'd be alone on a little island by myself. I be done cussed everybody out.

ROCHELLE: No friends. I think it's healthy to get mad. I think when we don't get mad about anything, that's really problematic and that's really unhealthy. 'Cause you're not allowing yourself to feel.

VERONICA: I felt though, I remember times with my friends before we went on spring break, I was consumed by anger. That was me. That was all that I was since the start of the semester. I was just an angry, walking attitude. Just constantly just mad. Mad every time I walked into the classroom. Mad every time I walked in my apartment because there's always a reminder of something. If I walk in the classroom, it's a reminder of what I got to deal with today or what I had to deal with last class. 'Cause I don't let stuff go. I'm not a grudge holder, but I remember. I always remember. I remember what you said and how you were and I'm not going to just, "Hey what's going on?" even though I hate you in the back of my mind. I can't do that. That's not how I live my life. I'm just not that type of people. I try to live my life in as much honesty as I possibly can and being fake, it's just too many things to keep track of so I feel what I feel and I react on what I feel and then I come home and the girl that I can't stand and I had all that drama with the first semester, she's right there. We share a bathroom. So no escape there. It's just like everywhere. I was just like, "I'm a nice person. I'm a good person to come to." I regard myself as being a person with a sense of humor. All those things about me that I know are positive, I had totally forgot. I was just mad. I was mad in my sleep. I was fighting in sleeping. I'm waking with scratches on my face. I was just always angry. I went home on the bus just tight, until I was able to go home and chill and not think about nothing. Then when I came back, I said, "Ooh no, this cannot happen to me." 'Cause I was getting physically ill. That gets to you. That emotional stuff. You start getting nauseous. I started losing my appetite. It was just affecting everything, every part of my life. That whole thing, when y'all said, remain optimistic. That's when that hit me. It's so important that I can't let everything consume me. It's not worth it.

Story Two:
I Know Me, Do You?: Identity and Black Women

. . . We must establish authority over our own definition, provide an attentive concern and expectation of growth which is the beginning of that acceptance we came to only expect from our mothers. It means that I affirm my own worth by committing myself to my own survival, in my own self and in the self of other Black women. (Lorde, 1996a, p. 173)

ROCHELLE: I feel passionate about being a Black woman. . . but it's hard and it's a daily struggle. . . I call it the daily struggle on the assault on my humanity. . . but how do you theorize away the pain. . . I want to know, how do my Black female students theorize away their pain? What do you even think your purpose is, as a Black woman?

VERONICA: That's a big question.

GRACE: It's huge. . . all I know is that it's huge. Given what I have, my home thing, everything with my family, I'm the go-to person and I'm 22 years old and even though my mom is a go-to person she's strong, takes on a lot of stuff, she's coming to me now. That's part of my purpose and that has a lot to do with me being a Black woman and my purpose on this earth.

VERONICA: Can I ask you something pertaining to that? You're the person that people depend on and you feel that as a Black woman that's part of your purpose. . . Do you feel that the fact that you are the person everybody depends on correlates with you being a Black woman?

GRACE: Yes! Because that's how we are.

VERONICA: Or is that how people have made us. . . because see I have a thing with them saying Black women are so strong. I'm no stronger than some White woman. I just think that Black women have learned to tolerate a lot of stuff so their level of tolerance is a lot higher than other people. The big thing we have to learn now is Black women need a point where they can be vulnerable; where people are not depending on them, let them depend on others for a change. They are human beings, they feel things, their hearts break. I watch my mother go from day to day to day like nothing was happening and then I hit 18 and I asked these questions. "You were doing that, that's what was happening when you closed your bedroom door that day or that's what was going on when you turned your face?" I never saw my mother shed a tear, nothing but yet this is everything that's was going on. "You mean you been dealing with this all by yourself" and she was socialized to be that way from the time she was a kid. A lot of Black women raised their mother's kid, Why? Because their mothers had to work two or three jobs at a time. So we are socialized to be strong. While that's a good quality, I'm not saying anything is wrong with that quality but I don't think that Black women should feel obligated to never say no.

There was a struggle with all of the women around issues of identity and what it meant to be a Black woman. They understood the burden of strength associated with Black women and also understood that Black women in general and their mothers in particular were strong because they had to be.

GRACE: I think what I'm struggling with every day is how society sees me, how I see myself through society's eyes and what I'm feeling inside. . .

Understanding this juxtaposition of the ways a person is constructed and the feelings inside served as a source of strength for Grace. The ability to think critically about her world was a calling card to survival. Green (1994) states that emancipatory thinking enables women to confront the ways in which they have constructed their social reality and to gain touch with their lived world.

CHINA: Yes! Just say it again.

GRACE: . . . I found myself struggling to be that strong woman. . . I got depressed, I needed to cry on somebody's shoulder. Every year since I was born till I came up here I was the go-to person for all my friends. Then it came down to I was starting to fall apart, like I needed somebody.

VERONICA: But when you need somebody where do you go?

CHINA: Who's there, nobody but yet you can be up till 4, 6 in the morning but. . . ?

VERONICA: "My man's over here, I'm gonna have to call you back." I've been dropped for so many people's man.

CHINA: And it's like "you can do it you're strong."

GRACE: But I'll tell you where my struggle lies because I said seeing myself through society's eyes because I wouldn't let them know so it came down to the point that I was breaking down. I wouldn't tell them because I could handle it, I had it all under control. Back to my purpose, my purpose is trying to be at that point where I am spiritually at peace with my self, I can understand that. . . just the understanding of it all. 'Cause I use to ask questions like why? when I was young. And I'm saying young as far as young-minded and in my soul like a couple years ago. Why this happened and why that happened, why they act this way. . . I can't do anything about that. All I can do is control how I react to it. . . So that's my purpose, trying to put all this together dealing with, like we were talking about society's eyes, the strong Black woman and bringing that to reality for me.

Disconnection from self forces Grace to deal with many things alone, thinking she does not or cannot need anyone, or she is unable to reach out and ask.

VERONICA: And doing that, you have to find a happy medium between still being that person that you wanna be and find those moments where you have to be selfish and the hell with everyone else. I got to worry about me. And I have a big problem also with finding that place, that happy medium. 'Cause I find myself making myself feel better by allowing others to lean on me.

CHINA: Everything y'all are saying is on the money!

VERONICA: If I can put myself in somebody else's life for five minutes and forget about my problems, that's my escape. . . . My father calls me codependent because he'll ask me how's your life and I'll go well my cousin and her and the baby blah, blah, blah and my best friend blah, blah, blah and he'll be like "I asked about you and your life. How are you doing? But you telling me about everybody, your mom, school, your cousins, but how's life with you?" Most I can say is "It's alright."

GRACE: But is it?

VERONICA: No! But how do you voice that and while I would love for Black women to be able to be vulnerable I am afraid to be vulnerable because people use that vulnerability against you. Especially in a position where you supposed to be the strong person. And once you become vulnerable it scares the hell out of others because "If *you* are vulnerable then where am I suppose to go?"

ROCHELLE: Okay, let me interrupt. Do you think showing your vulnerability as a Black woman. . .

CHINA: Depreciates almost what she's trying to stand for. . .

VERONICA: It's a sign of weakness.

CHINA: It's to the point. . . okay let me break it down on some real shit. . . It's the fact that we don't allow people to see that side of us. It becomes our own power trip. . . and people are constantly coming to us for problems, if we are constantly assisting people, in our own way it boosts our self-worth because we are helping others. As soon as we are seen as not the all knowing because we all have faults, but y'all know where I'm coming from. But as soon as they see that "Y'all don't know everything or have the answers to everything." As soon as we are not that then we, because especially people like us can see what other people are seeing, almost hear people's thoughts, you began to see they are almost looking at us like a child and a lot of a time—it is a common complex among Black women, that nurturing. We can't help our own children. I'm beginning to see, besides my man I'm with now, because we been together three years and there are other guys in my life 'cause we have an open relationship. . . my ex-man that I was with forever he got locked up. I was going to Rikers, I was baking cookies, I was sending him letters. And then I met another guy and he got locked up and I was sending him letters, I was being supportive, I was being that wife. . .

VERONICA: Girl, you got a little cycle going with you!

CHINA: That's okay; everyday I ask [in a mock whining voice], "is it in me?" I have to constantly be around people who need me. . . I feel better when I can help others but then I'm wondering am I feeling better because I'm helping them. . .

GRACE: You're helping yourself.

VERONICA: I've done that. Because I'm a person who pushes my help on people. Like granted they do come to me, especially here it's pretty much an open door. "Anytime you need to talk its not a problem." My old roommate from New York. . . "Call me if you need to call me collect then no problem I'll call you back." I didn't get no return on that.

STEPHANIE: It's a cycle. . .

VERONICA: I'm afraid of looking weak. That's my biggest fear. I don't like shedding a tear in front of anybody and I'm a big cry baby, I'd have to go in my room. Put the pillow over my face and cry. I just have a big. . . and I guess it has a lot to do with being a Black female because once somebody sees you weak can I ever get that position back as a strong woman?

CHINA: But you know why that correlates with being a Black woman because White women are looked at as being weak. . . somebody is always covering and hovering. . . like they are constantly being catered to. . . White girls in classes they just blend. . . We are not like that, we can't blend. I've seen so many things in my life as a *Black Woman*, just the daily struggle that I don't want to blend. We dealing with so many issues, Miss Rochelle. . . I can't even state what the problem is but then I want to feel like them, just put my feet up, I wish I could then my head wouldn't hurt. I wouldn't feel so heavy. . .

GRACE: I can't imagine that I don't have to go to work, I don't have to worry about paying no bills. All I have to do when I come to here is study. Oh, God! Can you imagine?

CHINA: But then I notice the White race is on its own path to self-destruction. . . killing themselves with technology. They quick to point out that we killing each other and maybe our shit is out in the air because people can look at us like our own little species and dissect us apart but nobody is pulling their shit out. They are killing themselves in their own ways. Them White girls don't eat, their inner turmoil that they can't talk about . . . they dealing with when there is not a problem you almost create one.

Black is something to be dissected, discussed, analyzed, and theorized away. These women expressed needing a wholeness about their self and fighting to find and keep that wholeness.

The conversation shifts to images of Black women in popular culture

VERONICA: See now I don't take stuff like that as personal. I don't know if I'm correct in this or maybe when I move further in my consciousness I will be offended. I separate myself from those women because I find those women in all races and the way in which they portray them, of course I believe there should be more of a balance. I do see videos now that portray women in a better light. I don't know, I don't get a twinge when I see those videos.

CHINA: You know what did it for me. I can almost separate myself and I would like to point out the fact that being from Brooklyn I'm always up on the newest style. I'm the first one to come to a party in something little 'cause I'm only going to be this young and fly once in my life and I don't forget that part in my Black consciousness. . . It's the fact that this is what did it for me. . . this new roommate. . . she's White but she's a feminist so we can have a lot of common ground, and she's very passionate about being a woman. Now of course it's on a different level than being a Black woman but she's very feisty, she'll jump up in a moment if we see something on TV. Like she's quick to show me a *New York Times* article, show me why it's wrong, so she's on that level so I can feel her. . . because before I was more like just being Black, being a woman was secondary and I love my own femininity.

So I was straight with not dealing with this woman thing and how I'm being slighted on a whole 'nother slant and you know you almost want one curve ball at a time. Like can I just catch one and deal with it. I mean I'm like this, HELP, so when I was watching MTV and they had that hip hop week and there was one with Mary J Blige, Foxy. Did you see the one with the guys?. . . and I know you feel me Veronica and they started talking about how they play women, yeah we fuck fans then they began to be collective and like. . . was like yeah, them groupies are good for something. What's the word?

ROCHELLE: Misogynistic.

CHINA: Yeah, misogynstic air and that's when I began and after seeing it as I watched other videos and I began to go hmmm. Before I was quick to be the one, "You go girl, she looks cute in her little outfit," or whatever and then I began to see things differently and I'm not quite getting offended, fully here [pointing to stomach] gut offended yet but I'm feeling it brew.

Students have a difficult time dealing with theory and critical thinking. When asked to critically deconstruct concrete aspects that are part of their daily reality like music videos or television programs they have a better understanding of critical thought. hooks states, "Teaching theory, I find that students may understand a particular paradigm in the abstract but are unable to see how to apply it to their lives. Focusing on popular culture has been one of the main ways to bridge this gap." (1990, p. 6)

ROCHELLE: It's not just getting offended. You guys know I love *ER*. . . I know in watching *ER* they misrepresent Black people, they have negative portrayals of Black people, especially Black women. . . I still am able to watch *ER* but also deconstruct *ER*.

VERONICA: Yeah, I think like you said I would look at those flyers like you showed us for our final last semester. I would take that, I could deconstruct that and it reminded me of hip hop videos and I deeply deconstructed that with no problem. Saw all the problems in it and I do have a problem with them advertising parties that way, using our butts to get people to come, with the rump shaker party they had earlier this semester. . . . Yeah, I did have a problem with it.

Hearing what others said forced Veronica to reevaluate her earlier assertion that representations of Black women in music videos did not bother or offend her.

GRACE: I don't think like that. It doesn't get me. I don't have enough energy or time to think about and to feel it down here. I mean I don't have the energy so I don't feel that way but in the same token I know there's a lot of Black females who are 22 years old and they have not even began to do the soul searching to think about their purpose as a Black woman that I have. That's why. . . I was telling Rochelle the other day about how my mother is and she is 52 years old and there are things she will not talk about because she doesn't want to know about herself in that manner. That's tragic to me. How can you not know? I am the one self-help queen. I love self-help everything. I love spiritual. I love getting to know myself, all that. I love it.

ROCHELLE: You know I finally bought one of her books [Iyanla Vanzant].

VERONICA: Which one?

ROCHELLE: *Value in the Valley of the Light.*

GRACE: That's what I'm saying, that's just me. My mom doesn't. . . and I know there's been a lot of struggles in her life. I know there are a lot of things that she's dealing with now and she won't talk about certain things, just about her. I'm trying to do that. It frightens me that as a 52-year-old woman, she cannot think about or deal with, cope with certain things. It frightens me that I have my cousin living with me in my house and she will not think about certain things that are vital to your survival. I don't get it. That's what I mean, it's sad.

CHINA: But you know what, Veronica brought it up, she made a really good point when she said, you can't force some people.

GRACE: I know.

CHINA: That's the most frustrating, but you can't.

VERONICA: But it's frustrating to watch it go on.

GRACE: Yeah it is. That's why I say sad because I know I don't get it, it's hard for me to understand that, but everybody's not the same person.

VERONICA: My mother—I want to say—is hard. My mother is 43 and she. . . I'll tell her stuff that I read, and she goes, "Yeah, see but that's not me, 'cause I was doing this and I was doing that. . ." and I'm like, "Explain it away, Mom." Then she goes to herself, once we get off the phone, and she really lets it register and then about two weeks later, she'll totally contradict everything she said on the phone with me. At that point it's absorbed. I know how to feed it to my Mom. I know she is gonna sit up there, she's gonna explain how this don't apply to her, and her life, and did this, and I only did it 'cause blah, blah, blah fifty million excuses and I'm like yeah, yeah, yeah, just remember what I told you. Go sit in your bed and think about it and then call me in two weeks and we'll talk about it later.

ROCHELLE: But you know, one of the things, you four, you're 21?

STEPHANIE: Twenty-two on Tuesday.

VERONICA: I'm 21.

GRACE: I'm 22.

CHINA: Twenty-one.

ROCHELLE: You guys are the exception. As far as your awareness, your level of awareness, as young African American women. Most women your age, whether they're on this campus or they're back home in our communities, not on a campus but out there working, don't have the level of awareness that you have. I think it boils down to education. I took my first Black history course in 1991 at the age of 33 and that's when I started getting angry. Like earlier, we were saying that you really got angry once you came up here or once you started taking my class or somebody else's African American history class. Then it's like, "Yeah, our life is really messed up." And there's some really intense social structures out there that are working to make sure that we as low as possible. You start really getting angry and the more you know, the angrier you get.

VERONICA: I see the whole Black consciousness thing. We all expecting, to me it's about, that's the thing, I don't have to like you, but we got a common 'cause. We got a common struggle and I'll be damned if I'm gonna let you go out for that by yourself. I might think you a bitch, I might not like you, I might want to kick your behind once we get behind closed doors, but if I see you gettin' beat down intellectually, emotionally, or whatever, by a group of people oppressing you because of something we have in common, like our color or our gender, I got your back.

CHINA: Thank you!

VERONICA: Even if I don't like you. We ain't got to, I ain't got to like my blood sister, but I got her back.

CHINA: There aren't people like you.

VERONICA: When you get in a situation, like she said, the whole Black consciousness, if they had that, then they would be there. They would have your back. They would be loyal to you. We ain't got to be friends, but I just don't understand how, in this generation, we just don't. . . it kills me. I tell my mother all the time, I think I was born at the wrong time. I think I should have been born back there with y'all, you know, because at least. . . my mom told me she was born and plenty of groups she did not like half them females. People was still sleeping with people's man and all that craziness going on, but when it came time for action and they had to march for something or they had to fight for something or they had to raise money for something, they did it. Then when it was over, somebody might have had a fight around this neighborhood, somebody might have been knocking on somebody's door to give them a good beat down, but the cause was first. That's my whole thing. The cause is first.

CHINA: I think also the fact that, but our cause is so watered down. It's almost to where people say our generation is so spoiled. We've had the. . . our parents fought, like our parents were marching.

GRACE: I hate when people say that.

CHINA: But they were. And now we're left with, the cause is still there because, yes they marched, and maybe Senate signed a bill, or they put this into action so yes, there were causes for. . . but the whole social element of it, things that you can't write down and bills that can't be passed and issues that aren't that easy to articulate still haven't been dealt with. We're dealing with it on a whole other, funny, strange level. I think it's hard for other generations to understand that. What our issues are as opposed to theirs, 'cause theirs was so blatant and ours are more subtle.

ROCHELLE: . . . even like when I gave the class. . . you know, I can never get classes to read, I don't know what it is. I struggle with this every semester.

VERONICA: They still don't read?

CHINA: We got screamed on.

VERONICA: She screamed on us too but I was doing my reading so I didn't care.

CHINA: I bought my book that day. Remember Miss Rochelle they didn't have the book so I brought my receipt and waved it in class saying I'll bring the book in on Thursday.

ROCHELLE: It's like they have a different book, remember you guys had *Aren't I a Woman?* They have *A Shining Thread of Hope* which is a Black woman's history. . . This goes from slavery to like maybe the '80s. It's a wonderful book and I got so mad with the students one day 'cause I had this nice. . . I had been up till three in the morning planning, you know I never plan lectures. I had actually planned a lecture. I was ready. I had questions. I went to class; three-fourths of the class didn't have the book. I was mad. I was so pissed.

GRACE: She was pissed.

ROCHELLE: I started reading from. . . two semesters ago I had this book, *We Are Your Sisters* which had actual writings by enslaved women. I started reading about slave women sneaking off to learn how to read and things that folks would do for education with the fear of death hanging over their head. I'm like you guys are not even taking advantage of what is offered to you and taking education for granted. Let's not even go way back to slavery, let's just go to the '60s, with people marching and fighting and dying just so you could sit in State and go to college or so affirmative action bills could get passed or whatever and the generation today not taking advantage of that. . . Kids today don't know about those struggles. They don't know and care about the struggles that we went through in the past. Where does that fault lie? It can't just lie. . . it's like there's no panacea; it's never one thing that is the problem. If the generation today doesn't understand the problem, then it's gotta be not only their fault, but it's gotta be. . .

GRACE: I think a lot of it has to do with the fact that people think its over and it's far from over.

CHINA: It's almost the year 2000 so get over it. You okay now.

GRACE: All the marches, the protest were for more than us to go into the restaurant it was more than that. . .

VERONICA: I think it has something to do with. . . Personally my friends, people I grew up with, we all had drama. There was not time to teach people about Black history or empowerment. My ma just had enough strength to listen to me talk about my day in school and act like she was paying attention. We all had drama, all of us. It is so deep to see me and my five girlfriends talk about our childhood. We didn't have no money, everybody living in the ghetto, surrounded by drugs, surrounded by drug addicts. Whether they be in your house or at your front door there was so much that by the time I got to the age I was lucky because my mother got me out of the situation and me and her got a rap to the point I was so keen on who she was and she respected me for who I was that I had the power to make my own choices, not everybody has that, a mom who has their back.

> The reality of Veronica's childhood was that she got out of a bad situation. But growing up in "drama" and with a strong supportive mother allowed Veronica to realize her luck and also to want to do something for others. Veronica was not just achieving for herself, but for her mother and those kids who were still caught up in the "drama."

CHINA: My brain hurts.

ROCHELLE: There was an article we read in the class *Racism and Sexism* and Yamato called racism a mind-funk. Like you said your mind hurts, you just pissed, you tired and your mind hurts. And that's what racism will do, this intense, dehumanizing mind-funk where you are tired and your mind hurts and you just trying to maintain your sanity and trying to get from point A to point B to hell with point D and E you just trying to get to B.

CHINA: And also trying to get there with a little bit of style and a little bit of class about yourself. And almost on the element of still trying to have fun with it, dealing with all of these issues still make it look neat. It's getting difficult to do my makeup you know as you become more aware it almost becomes more of a hassle. It's a chore to put my lipstick on it's not even fun because my mind is not with it.

Story Three:
Just Take a Breath: Survival and Black Women

What other creature in the world besides the Black woman has had to build the knowledge of so much hatred into her survival and keep going? (Lorde, 1996a, p. 150)

GRACE: Can we talk about, like something to go along with that as far as the being positive part? Where, how do we draw lines as Black women? How do we, 'cause I've been really fighting with this because my friend, I love her to death, she's my best friend in the whole wide world. She was there for me. She's just my heart, my sister, my soul, whatever you want to say, that's my girl. But she's driving me crazy! She is driving me crazy because we have this relationship where she is, and I'm sure she thinks that she gives all of herself to me and I do believe she does, but at the same time, I'm giving a lot to her and I can't really, I can't do it anymore and try to graduate? I can't right now, I just cannot do it. So where do you and how do you draw a line in your relationship, day to day in what you do as a Black woman? Not just saying about saying no. Because we can't say no. I'm not just saying about, no I'm not gonna do that, the power to say no. I'm not saying that. I'm saying more so just drawing a line where your friends, family, people, your loved ones, people you care about, people who are in your life, can step and not step. They just can't pass that. Do you guys know?

VERONICA: Where their issues and problems will consume your life you mean?

GRACE: No, not even that. That. . .

CHINA: Where that severance of the connection is and where you just deal with it. . . and then say. . .

GRACE: Yes, Yes.

When you give so much of your Self to others little is left for you. The question that Grace asked, "Where do you draw the line?" is a difficult one to answer and like many things there is no one answer. The line between self and others and how much can you give while still remaining whole is fluid and these women were struggling with how to move within that fluidity instead of confining self to a small fixed space.

GRACE: It's so liquid. Yes, that's what I'm saying. It's so hard. I don't, I try to, I was reading Iyanla the other day and she was saying, actually that was one of my things that I had to do in one of the days and I couldn't do it. I was really, I was depressed about trying to do it 'cause I was. . .

ROCHELLE: What stops you from doing it?

GRACE: Past relationships, just how I've dealt with stuff in the past and then my ability to say, "Don't you think that was a little much?" or "What gives you the right to say that to me?" or "What gives you the right to. . ." I guess because, it's even more than that. I never drew the line with her in the first place, I don't think. I never said, "Ok, well this is mine, this is yours and this is where I'm not gonna let you come into my life and this is where I'm gonna let us deal with these problems together. And this is what I'm gonna share with you and this is what I'm gonna share. This is gonna be this little space that's mine or this big space that's mine." I don't think I've really done that, especially when you keep letting people in and keep letting in and I'm saying not more people, but I'm saying like one person, the more you love them, the more they're in your life. As far as my girlfriend, she, the more I show her and I give her and I share with her, but I don't have a space to say. . .

". . . there is a middle depth of interaction possible and sustainable, an emotional limit to relationships of self upon self acknowledged" (Lorde, 1996a, p. 163).

ROCHELLE: Do you think it goes back to what you guys, what we were all talking about earlier with like, as Black women, feeling that we've gotta be strong, we've gotta be there for other people. Part of our personality is nurturing. We nurture other people and that if we're not there, how. . . I think somebody here said it, like if we're not there for other people, then that kind of takes away from who we are? Was that you, China, who said that? Ok. Could that be part of the reason why you don't know how to draw that space? Is it the space or just about self-preservation? Like you give so much of yourself that you have nothing left for. . .

GRACE: Yes. Yes.

ROCHELLE: It's like you're afraid to even say. . .

GRACE: . . . but I was taught that. That's what my mother does on a daily basis. She gives all of herself to everybody in my family. To me, my brother, my cousins and my aunts, uncles, and my grandma, everybody. She's spun. You know what I'm saying? That's what I know how to do. I don't think. . .

CHINA: But see the thing is that, 'cause that is my mother to the letter. It's just me and my mom, single parent without my dad. He tries to get in the picture, but basically I'm just through, you know what I mean? My mom, she's just on that whole, I feel you on that. Especially, I'm her only child, so it's just me and her. So really, at times in our house together, in our apartment, it's me and her against the world. We'll sit and talk for hours. It's really us against them. But what I'm beginning to realize, even from listening to other people explain how their mothers are like that, or their parents, I'm beginning to see and then relating it back to myself and then almost relating it back to you. I'm seeing so much of me in you, that I'm beginning to see that it's not, you almost wanna think that they're giving all of themselves and that they're getting nothing back, but really as they're giving all of themselves, they're getting back for that giving. For that nurturing and that, they're getting back that dependency, that codependence, to where my mom has it so that almost all her life, she has everything under control to where if she moves out of the way, a part of everybody's life will fall apart.

> *The dialectic between strength and weakness, helping others and hurting self is so strong for these women. At the same time that they reject the stereotypes and images they also buy into them. Ladson-Billings and Tate (1995) contend that a "factor contributing to the demoralization of marginalized groups is self-condemnation. Members of minority groups internalize the stereotypic images that certain elements of society have constructed in order to maintain their power." (p. 57)*

VERONICA: That is my life.

CHINA: It's almost like in that, it's power, because it's almost like if I were to drop dead, this would happen. Now it's not necessarily that conscious thing, no, that my mother is saying, "I have the whole family depending on me and it makes me feel better." It's all their subconscious, so I'm beginning to see it's a cycle that we have to hurry up and break now before we have our babies because it will be automatic. It will be automatic because as us being raised that way, that's what we know of as love. I know that if I love someone, I have to put myself in their shoes because my mother loves me. . .

ROCHELLE: Girl is about to preach.

CHINA: That's the only way I know how to love, so if I don't hurry up and find a way to fix it or to put it a different way, I'm gonna do the same thing with my kids as soon as I have kids. I can feel that maternal, as soon as I have my babies I'm gonna give them everything. I'm just gonna, and then the cycle perpetuates and they see, well mommy did that, and then that's why I'm hoping maybe staying married or being able to have a family and sort of help to have a father figure there to almost help put a little of the weight. . .

GRACE: Share, yes.

CHINA: You need to almost share the battles, but I don't even know how to. I almost don't know how to, in all the ways that I'm very feminine, I don't know how to have that, that whole, how Tupac says, "There's a thug in the house, now you can rest. Lay your tired head on my chest." That whole, I almost don't know how to do that because I've never seen anybody lay their head. I've never seen my mother lay her head anywhere except on a pillow next to me. T. D. Jakes talks about that. Children being their mother's husband. I can see how I'm almost her husband. You know, "Mom did you pay the bill. Mommy, don't put the. . ." Yes, and we almost share it like a husband. My mom will tell me what happened at her job. You know, we share almost, it's almost bordering on almost a funny, undescribable, romantic type, it's almost on that whole. . .

> *"How do we love another and still love ourselves?" was a concern for all of the women.*

VERONICA: Can I ask a question, too? Is it also because, I find that, OK, my mother's always been like that. She's just now, she's just maybe in late 30s or early 40s learned to be selfish. Handles. . .but she says no. But look how late it took her. But I want to ask, is it partly because, like the love thing, I totally understand that, but is partly because you don't trust nobody to do it besides you? You know what I'm saying? If you got all these people depending on you, got all these people coming to you, if all of sudden these people did not come to you and they decided to do it on their own and you heard about them do-ing it alone, I'm just going from my mother. She's like, "You gonna mess up." Like, "No, let me do it, let me do it." Writing checks to pay my rent. I'm like calm your nerves, I can write a check. Or did you, one time she said, "Do you remember your address?" I'm like I'm just gonna be 18? To that point where you are so, you can do it, all the work that if you just put your hands up for two seconds, you feel like the world is gonna fall apart. I think that's why you can't let it go.

GRACE: I don't know. I've never thought about it. I can see, when you're talking. . . about my mom, I can see that in her, but I don't know. I don't think I know anything else, to tell you the truth. I think that I've always. . .

CHINA: I want to know how to do it.

VERONICA: That's my point.

CHINA: I want to know how to be. . .

Woman-child. As much as they are young women still growing and feeling for their wings they are also women in the fullest sense of the word. They are taking responsibility for their lives, their families, and their communities. In many ways they are fulfilling the role Black women have always played in the community.

VERONICA: You know how to be. . . 'cause I'm a person that people depend on a lot, but Veronica always takes time for herself. Now I don't know if that's because I'm my mother's only child and I have, I just have these moments of selfishness where I'm just like. . .

CHINA: Oh girl, yes, you know, I gotta have the spotlight.

VERONICA: I don't call it selfishness.

CHINA: I do.

VERONICA: I don't, I have my time.

GRACE: It's about me.

VERONICA: But I don't call it selfish. You have to cultivate that time then.

GRACE: It's just like I said, I'm a self-help, the books, I'm all about grow-ing, and myself and pushing on as far as myself, like helping myself whatever.

VERONICA: But when you are with yourself.

GRACE: Yes.

VERONICA: It seems so intense all the time, you know what I'm saying like you said about self-help, the books, you about this. . . Your time by yourself has got to chill sometimes.

ROCHELLE: At the beginning of the semester I had a meeting with my three TA's about what to do for the semester and Grace is gettin' stressed out. I could see her, you could see her gettin' stressed, it was like her head was throbbing. I said, Grace, this is supposed to be fun. . . But like Veronica is saying you do take everything on a real serious level.

VERONICA: I can give this advice but I don't take it myself. I always got headaches. . . I'm trying to watch stupid TBS movies, I'm in them to just not remember.

GRACE: I do have my veg time, that's why I read my fiction books but that's what I don't want anymore. I want to be able to sit down and commonly look at whatever not to escape anything you know what I'm saying because I do that. I watch TV and I don't feel any stress, I'm cool, but at the same time I want to be able to sit and think about my life, the people around me and not be intense, not think about this and how it affect this; why is that hard?

VERONICA: We are at an age when we are, hey. . . we are at a big question-mark point in our life. We don't know what's going to happen. We can have the best plans, the best grades, the perfect major, I still don't know what to do with my life. Are we talking personal, professional if we got problems with our families are those problems gonna be resolved is just a bit question mark. Everywhere we turn it's a question. . . because we are at a very intense point in our lives and I don't think there is anything we can do until we have some answers. I don't know if that's gonna help because it's not solving anything but I'm telling you that I think we are all in the same boat because if we care at all about what our future holds it's gonna be intense because we don't know and we wanna know and we are also women who wanna be in control so if you don't it's frustrating, period.

CHINA: Maybe that's why we are also into our own Black consciousness and like Miss Rochelle said the beginnings of the attempts at awareness and maybe that's what helps us to be not necessarily better people, not better than other people, but in certain instances in wanting to be in constant control we began to, we are at least taking charge of being in control of ourselves. We are and now you are at that sorta crossroads where you are branching and having growing pains and in that pain there is so much growth that people are. . . you're helping and they are not giving it back. . .

ROCHELLE: And looking at Grace's question where do we draw the line I think first we have to realize that we deal with it from our personality so we figure out that line accordingly and figure out when I'm doing something and giving something to somebody and I'm taking away from myself. I'll do as much as I can but when it gets to the point that I'm giving so much of myself that I am no longer Rochelle. . .

CHINA: How do you know when you get to that point, does it come with age, when you get older can you almost predict when that's gonna come up? I've seen it happen to me but it's almost too late I've got caught up and I've had to make that severance and sometimes you have to burn bridges. . . and that person on the other end doesn't see that you are trying to bring yourself back into you. They go off and then they're mad when do you almost make the severance easier by seeing it sooner?

ROCHELLE: No longer can I give one year or two years of my life and I think we do know on some level when we are being used, when we are giving so much of ourselves. You know when talking to somebody about their problems you should be doing. . . it's like accepting that we know.

GRACE: You really know, the voice warns you that you have to get up.

ROCHELLE: Negative friends. . .

VERONICA: All that negative energy.

CHINA: What is it that T.D. Jakes said, "To soar with eagles you have to leave the pigeons alone.". . . Leave them alone. . . and what is it that my mother says, "Slime will seek its own level" it's not content until everybody is level with it. Oh no, my mom and I are very into. . . but then on the other hand you find yourself not totally alone but just around those few powerful profound people. Because I am learning that it almost sickens me to be around people that can't be here with me. Its almost very obnoxious of me to say that but screw it but that works for me, people that are constantly on a negative or just that blinder level, it gives me a headache it brings me down and I can almost feel them wanting to bring me down.

ROCHELLE: Those people who are our true friends or true lovers they know. . .

CHINA: PREACH!! You notice everybody, is it just me or do people just in general just want to change you? I always feel like people want to change me. Do you find that Miss Rochelle? I feel like just about everybody I have encountered in my life are trying to change me somehow. Like why can't people just leave me alone? You know I wish everybody would just leave me alone, White people just leave me alone, just leave me alone!

VERONICA: It's why do they even come around? If you don't like who I am, why you come around?

GRACE: Don't try to hold me. You know what I mean. I'm trying to go places and be somebody. Trying to hold me in one spot, not so much trying to change me but. . .

CHINA: Yeah, Yeah.

GRACE: In that little box.

CHINA: And it almost drives you crazy trying to get out of it and you feel bad and you're wondering when should I just stay there? Just leave me alone, you can quote me on that. . . I'm feeling like I'm being picked on. Like everybody is picking on me in some way or the other. If I was to grovel in it I would have pity parties every night. But actually just sitting here talking about it tonight the overall feeling I have just by society, by everybody, I just feel picked on. You know nobody will leave me alone. Just let me live. I mean I'm not asking for much you know from the overall general White society. I mean I'm asking to be equal but they'll never see me as that but that's what I'm trying to get to.

VERONICA: Do you think we'll ever get there?

CHINA: With equal?

VERONICA: Yeah

CHINA: No, no.

VERONICA: I hate to sound pessimistic but I don't know.

GRACE: I don't think so either.

ROCHELLE: There's this guy Derrick Bell and he wrote this book *Faces at the Bottom of the Well: The Permeance of Racism* and what he talks about is the fact that racism is always going to be part of American society. I mean America was built on racism, people are comfortable with it, and it's not going to leave. Therefore, instead of teaching this "We are the world," we need to teach how to deal with racism. So how do you deal within that and still achieve and still maintain your humanity, still feel beautiful, still feel intelligent because you know media and all of this other shit will keep you down.

VERONICA: Racism is not going to go away in my lifetime.

CHINA: It will never disappear because it's too embedded in our society, it's too deep.

ROCHELLE: And as long as we have racism that means somebody wins and somebody loses and of course we are the ones who lose and people are not going to give up.

CHINA: . . . they will never give up winning.

CHINA: Well, Miss Rochelle you said on the phone we were going to discuss survival strategies and ways to survive everyday life. It ties in perfect with what you just said about the book. Like what were some of his suggestions, what are some of your suggestions or just techniques? What is working, what are you doing?

ROCHELLE: Teaching. . . educating myself and helping to educate my students.

CHINA: But I'm talking about day-to-day life on the streets say if somebody clutches their purse in the mall when nobody comes to help you, just little stuff that gets you to almost explode.

They wanted and needed a recipe book for dealing with racism. If A happens, then do B or proceed immediately to E. If only such a book with concrete examples existed.

GRACE: I was in Ben and Jerry's and I was looking through *Essence* and *Ebony* and I had put the magazines down and there was a family, little boy and girl, White family, and I'm standing there going between. . . trying to decide which one my poor ass can afford. So I am sitting there, I had the *Ebony* in my hand and the *Essence* for April has the face of a Black woman on the cover. It's not even her body just her face, it's like real big. This family is looking at me and I'm like why are they looking at me. I'm like what the hell. And then the mother is trying to play it off and she's like her glasses are nice, I'm like whatever. Then I'm reading my book not even paying attention but I felt a vibe that was weird. So I'm reading it and then they're leaving and the *Essence* is on the table. So, he's going by and he hits the *Essence*, like smack. And I'm like and I didn't know how to take it.

CHINA: How old was he?

GRACE: Like eight or nine. He was old enough to know what he was doing. And I didn't know what to do. I stood there and looked at the mom like what?. . . and then I had to calm down, I had to literally calm down and I was saying like he hit the magazine. I took it away from where my mind went to take it.

CHINA: So what did the mother do?

GRACE: They left, she didn't do anything. The boy left, everybody left, and I didn't turn around because I didn't. . .

CHINA: That's what I mean like what do you do to survive, that's like every day.

ROCHELLE: One of the things we were saying earlier is that you can't get pissed off at everything or you'll be pissed off all the time. I mean, you can be angry and you can be upset but what can you do? Chase the woman down, back her up against the wall, and educate her.

VERONICA: And have the police come and you're like, "Officer, I was just educating her."

CHINA: . . . when they push us "Why do you all have to have your own this, this and this?" It's well, first off you brought us over here and we didn't want to be here in the first place. But then when we do try to assimilate after we're emancipated y'all don't let us into anything and then when we try to make our own stuff y'all not happy. I'm coming to grips with my own caring less and less and less with what the greater society thinks about me. You know, and trying to do that is hopefully going to help me control my anger because you only get angry about the things you feel passionate about and care about. So obviously when I get mad it's because I care about what they're thinking or I'm caring almost what people are thinking about me that I don't need to care about. And that's my own little survival strategy if you care less about what they're thinking and you'll be less angry. Does that make sense?

ROCHELLE: Perfect sense.

To remain whole you sometimes have to disassociate yourself from those things and people who seek your destruction. China realized this and also realized that it was something she had to remind herself of daily.

GRACE: I breathe.

CHINA: Everybody's been telling me to breathe lately. Where do you have to breathe, in your nose, out your mouth, what's the best, most effective way to breathe?

GRACE: That's basically it, just breathe. Just take it in.

CHINA: I really don't know. I really don't breathe, that's part of my problem.

GRACE: I know it helps me 'cause that's what I did whenever the boy did that, I was like, just breathe. You know what I'm saying? I just took in, felt what I was feeling and breathed it up.

CHINA: I need to learn how to breathe.

VERONICA: I'm just saying that seems too simple, but. . .

CHINA: It helps you to breathe too?

VERONICA: My feelings are so intense. When I feel them, they're so, so intense.

GRACE: Now, I didn't say that I had lost the moment or I lost all my feelings with that one breath, but it did take me, in that moment, yes. It brought everything down.

ROCHELLE: It grounded you for a moment.

VERONICA: And after that?

GRACE: It let him walk out. For me not to snatch him up.

The women gather the pieces of themselves that sista dialogue allowed to be made visible. They had been in a safe space for being and feeling who they were, at least for six hours. They all hug me, wish me luck with my book. They embrace each other, exchange phone numbers with promises of keeping in touch.

The end.

Reflection

"I really don't breathe, that's part of my problem"

The women of sista dialogue were my spiritual sisters and my spiritual children. They represented that part of me that wraps itself in the need to teach, the need to provide direction toward empowerment for my students. I raised internal questions that needed answers. I hoped that those answers would lead me to more questions and better answers. I was the Socratic method in mind and body. I wanted to enmesh myself in a cycle of understanding. Partake in a journey of growth. To bring into being a recipe for life and teaching. I believed that if I could ferret out the strategies these young Black women had developed to remain whole I would be able to find the answers, the solutions to issues that have plagued Black women since time begin for us in the U.S. I hoped that I would find my place, my influence on their development.

I remembered and relived the words of Kahil Gibran's *The Prophet*. If a teacher is "indeed wise he does not bid you enter the house of wisdom, but rather leads you to the thresh hold of you own mind" (Gibran, 1951/2004, p. 56) and "the vision of one man lends not its wings to another man" (Gibran, p. 57). As their teacher I never intended for my students to parrot my beliefs. Instead I wanted to bring them to a place of voice where they would believe in limitless possibilities because they came to understand that within each of their beings there resided boundless creativity and resourceful intelligence. Each were "[t]he sons and daughters of life's longing for itself" (Gibran, p. 17) and if they believed in the wisdom that was part of their ancestral past the world could be theirs.

Listening to the women of Sista Dialogue discuss their Black femaleness was an organic experience for me. The honesty, the anger, the laughter, the fear, the hope encircled their words and thoughts until eight women became one voice. And I do not mean one voice as if their was no individuality between them but the common experience of being Black and female and in tune with each other led to a strong voice that was as separate as it was one. There was a syncopation that existed—a bittersweet melody—which the women sang so clearly that while there was unison you could also hear each distinctive voice. They struggled to find the answers for each other to questions that constructed their identity.

Did I answer any of the plethora of questions I posed at the onset of this study? Yes and I also got answers to questions I didn't ask. Finally, as I hoped, through their dialogue the women forced me to think of new questions that as of yet have no answers.

An overarching question in my study was what were the opposing forces these Black women struggled against in their rise to a political and social consciousness? As I have stated elsewhere in this book the women of sista dialogue were chosen specifically because of their positionality in the search for a Black feminist consciousness. They were searching for self, questioning who they were and importantly who they wanted to become. Veronica stated that "[w]e are at a big question-mark point in our life. We don't know what's going to happen…everywhere we turn it's a question." China replies they are at the "beginning of their attempts at awareness and maybe that's what helps." Although the questions they had about life were big the women understood that the answers were not going to come without time and work. In order to *figure out* answers they needed to both lean on their accumulated knowledge and to have faith in self. Each woman acted as a mirror, a reflection into the soul of the other women. They built a community of transformation during the six hours of sista dialogue.

Within that community the women tackled the many parts that made up their identity. A significant part of the early conversation was what we do when we are finally confronted with our race. Although each woman encountered the issue of race in different ways and at different moments in their lives a commonality exists in their shared anger. The words of Veronica articulated the thoughts of all of the women: "I am now getting pissed and I think that's why I'm so frustrated because it's all smacking me in the face, like every day, like constantly." Veronica grew up in an all-Black inner-city community and stated that race was something she was not confronted with or consciously thought about until she arrived at State. She went on to say that her childhood was filled with so much turmoil that her life was about daily survival. At the time she could not understand the ways race constructed her realities and those of her mother. Trying to survive the onslaught of life takes up much of the time of what Gwaltney (1993) calls Drylongso—common people. Paying the bills, getting the job, working overtime, raising the children, living life leaves little time to try to deconstruct the meanings of life. For some of us in the academy we do it for a living but for those folks in the *real* world the specialized knowledge needed or the time to sit and think is not a part of their reality. The information people need to have to be able to truly understand the forces that dominate them and construct their life is not readily available in schools, the church or the media—the three institutions that people come into contact with more often.

Once the women of sista dialogue started college and began to take classes that provided the necessary information they became angry. Again Veronica states, "I was mad in my sleep. I was fighting in my sleep. It's so important that

I not let everything consume me." When you begin to see what is attempting to hold you and your race down anger is often the first emotion that results. The anger is grounded in the knowledge that you have been lied to all of your life, made to feel that the problems of your community were justified because of the people in the community. You never knew the systemic structures, which were purposefully hidden from your view. Again I am reminded of *The Prophet* speaking on self-knowledge. He states that "The soul walks not upon a line, neither does it arrow like a reed. The soul unfolds itself, like a lotus of countless petals" (Gibran, 1951/2004, p. 55). Coming into knowledge is not linear. I always tell my students to think of knowledge as an onion (I am not as poetic as Gibran) and that like an onion they need to continuously peel off the layers of knowing to eventually arrive at the nugget of *truth*. China asserted, "Everything is starting to come together. I'm seeing the whole picture." But seeing the whole picture is frustrating. Trying to articulate what we feel inside is difficult. The emotion can cloud our words and our thoughts. For example, China stated that once she began to understand there was a feeling of helplessness and that she needed "somebody else there to almost argue for me because [she] almost felt out of [her] league, like [she] had stepped beyond what [she] could almost argue."

The new ways of seeing that knowledge provides was evident in one of the assignments I give my students, a TV log that they keep for a week while watching a variety of television programs and stations. They are required to use class discussions, readings, and films to analyze what they see. The students often report that before the assignment they never thought much about what was presented on television but after it they become critical of what's out there. It is so much easier to be oblivious to the crap that is shoved down our psyche daily. Once you see *it* everything is different. I needed my students to understand the nexus of race, class, and gender and that they must use their deeper understanding to demystify life. What seems innocent or innocuous is in reality quite nocuous.

For instance, during a portion of sista dialogue the women discussed how they were (or were not) dealing with the misogynistic depictions in the public mind of African American women. Needless to say we turned to music videos, which generally have the most negative depictions of Black women. Several of the women commented that they were just beginning to understand the misogyny that was in the videos. China mentioned that although she was "not quite there" she was nevertheless beginning to "see things differently." What was confusing to the women was why some women would subject themselves to that treatment for a few dollars or a few minutes of fame. Or better yet why singers like Foxy Brown or Lil' Kim would portray themselves in such a manner.

Internalized racism eats away at the individual because they do not know (or care) how their actions are not only hurting them but Black women in general. In a patriarchal, racist, capitalistic society the dollar is the Holy Grail and must be obtained by any means. The person is not necessarily concerned about their representation of a Black woman as an ass-shaking, hootchie-outfit-wearing, come-and-get-me sex toy. Worse yet because of miseducation they do not know how the image they are presenting in the 21st century relates to the image of Black women in the 20th century. The image (in their mind) has no relation to the continued devaluation and subjugation of Black women.

According to the women the strong Black woman image had the greatest influence on their identity. They easily saw and understood the connections between that image and how they, their mothers, and other Black women experienced life. The women questioned how to be strong and weak and simultaneously questioned their humanity. They understood that in a society that depicts Black women negatively is for some the most positive they can hold onto. For Grace the superwoman depiction of Black women resulted in her experiencing severe depression alone, afraid to confide in friends about what she was going through. She stated, "I wouldn't tell them because I could handle it, I had it all under control." Grace knew in her heart she didn't have it under control but she also believed that in a society that views depression as weakness and Black women as inhumanely strong, able to take it all that she could not afford to show weakness. After all who would understand? And as one of the women articulated if strength is all we have then when we admit frailty will I loose a large part of myself? Veronica asked the other women, "Do you feel that the fact that you are the person everyone depends on correlated with you being a Black woman?" So we are socialized to be strong.

All of the women admitted that a major direct influence on their identity was their mother. They accepted the positive influences of their mothers and questioned what they knew to be problematic. For example they saw that their mothers had bought into the concept of the strong Black woman and because of life circumstance took that strength as both a badge of honor and their central survival strategy. But the women pondered how to rest when they had never or seldom seen the women closest to them rest. According to China, "I've never seen anybody lay their head. I've never seen my mother lay her head anywhere except on a pillow next to me." Grace related how her mother gave everything of herself to everyone until there was very little left. She posed the question where to draw the line as Black women. The ever-thoughtful Veronica answered that "you have to find a happy medium between still being that person you wanna be and finding those moments where you have to be selfish and the hell with everyone else." Veronica also understood that helping others was a "power trip" as China stated because she felt better about self "by allowing others to lean on" her.

Viewed, as the nurturer Black women have to be careful not to become the *tit* of society. China admitted to having a series of jailbird boyfriends that she knew she could help if she loved them enough, visited them in prison enough, mothered them enough. Of course she also saw how she was losing herself in the process of helping the men find themselves. At the same time that China was giving little pieces of herself to men who were not worthy she was also demanding respect. One of her funniest comments occurred when we discussed a fight that occurred in class when she felt a Black male classmate had verbally disrespected her. Coming from Brooklyn (her words) China was not going to sit and take it. She asserted that "I'm not gonna be picked on. I'm not gonna allow everybody to sit up here and shit on me." If only she would use that same feistiness to make better decisions about whom she involved herself with. I believe it stems from the nurturer misnomer that we accept and allow to become part of us without thinking.

The six hours I spent with the women during sista dialogue I will always remember. They helped me in so many ways that I will never be able to completely articulate. Even though my study took place over four years ago I still think about the women, their words, how much of themselves they gave, what they taught me about myself. My final question in this project was what does all I have done, read, analyzed really have to do with discovering a *pedagogy of humanity* and evolving philosophy—creating wholeness in Black women?

My little soon-to-be-teacher was Carole. Of all of the women Carole's and Jennifer's background were the most economically privileged. Carole was also the youngest of all the women and although she had more world experience due to an extensive amount of traveling in some ways she was also one who was struggling the most with internalizing a Black feminist consciousness. Despite this I witnessed the intellectual work Carole forced herself to undertake. She truly wanted to understand the struggles of the other women and how they had reached the level of consciousness they were currently at. Carole taught me to develop in my curriculum an equal concentration on helping students develop specialized as well as organic knowledge. I also learned from Carole to be positive in the face of all that is wrong with the world. She showed great fortitude and perseverance in always trying to find the positive in negative situations. Carole asserted when talking about the mentor teachers in her student teaching experience that "in one aspect…it makes me frustrated by their words and tired, but then on the other hand, sometimes I'm like, if I'm not gonna do it who will? You see how much problems there are and…you can either become tired—and we are allowed to be tired once in a while because if you don't just take a break from it then we're gonna crumple ourselves, but I think it's good to see how much problems there are out there, it's also inspiration to go out and try to do something about it."

Stephanie was sweet and very shy. Her level of confidence was so low that often as her teacher I had to work on her comfort level in class and hope that whatever "concrete" information I was teaching she would somehow internalize. I learned from Stephanie that the best pedagogy I could develop must include work on the spirit of the students. Stephanie had to learn to trust me as her teacher, that I wouldn't hurt her and would try my best to protect her in class before she could open her mind up to the difficult and emotional information I was presenting. At the end of sista dialogue when asked what worked in my class for her, Stephanie stated, "I just started thinking about little things, I'm not gonna say little things just important things that I should have been thinking about that nobody taught me how to think about."

Natasha was perhaps the most self-assured student I had. It was this self-assuredness that allowed her to be the positive voice in the conversation. She realized the things she had going in her favor but rather than using them to place herself above the other women Natasha constantly attempted to place them within a valid context—not making herself less or dismissing the concerns of the other women. During a conversation about White standards of beauty and hair Natasha's hair was envied as being "good" to which she answered, "Everybody has a different texture of hair. Asian women have a different texture hair but they can use a product that a White woman would use. Gel, I don't have Dark and Lovely gel in my cupboard, or whatever. I use whatever is cheap." Natasha taught me to take my students from where they were and to not place my expectations on them. They were not to be molded in my image but to be there own people. I could provide students with whatever knowledge I possessed but I could not tell them how to use that knowledge. If I did my job right then what I gave them would be the tools and the responsibility to help others and make sure that their community benefited from what they knew and had.

Stacy possessed a great deal of commitment to helping other African Americans, especially children. Growing up in Haiti and allowing the experience of being African American and Haitian to be a major part of her identity forced Stacy to accept the responsibility of fostering in Black children a positive sense of self. She stated that "I know when I get up there with a degree or something, I'm gonna try to write books for little children. . . start early and then you can get something clear in their brains about. . . what's beautiful about different races. 'Cause in kindergarten, what I learned about Cat in the Hat and all that crap. . ." Stacy used her prior experiences to help her better understand what needed to be done now. She taught me to expand my knowledge of and commitment to Black people throughout the African Diaspora. Until I did so I was only partially helping my students achieve a transformative way of being because I was not attempting a comprehensive understanding of the Black experience.

Jennifer was in the middle of her master's program and student teaching during sista dialogue. She was also in the midst of coming to her own awareness about race and infusing that awareness in her teaching. Jennifer was concerned about the White teachers at State high school who denied race and racism and therefore were not helping children expand their worldview. She stated, "I think that's why it's so frustrating right now…I'm at the point where if it wasn't for me sitting in that room looking at these faces…that's what causes me to lose sleep. I try to be optimistic. I came in here. I know I was going into a predominantly White setting, and I get in here and I'm teaching these kids and I'm like, all right, I'm showing them they gotta have a worldview. . ." What I saw on the outside of Jennifer was not who she was. As her mentor I assigned Jennifer to a preconceived specific box based on who I imagined her to be and by doing so did her a grave injustice. Jennifer taught me to look deeper into each of my students, open my mind and heart so the person could show me who they truly were on the inside.

The maturity and intensively internal nature of Grace taught me that as students move further into their consciousness the questions become more difficult for them to deal with and for me to answer as their teacher. If the question asked is the right one the answer will not only be difficult but will change with time and place. Grace stated that she struggled with her identity. She said, "What I am struggling with every day is how society sees me, how I see myself through societies eyes and what I'm feeling inside." Grace was also the student I had known the longest and seen grow from someone who attempted to separate her Blackness from every other part of her being to someone who put it first when defining self. I have every confidence that Grace will become the woman she wants to be because as she says her purpose is to be "where I am spiritually at peace with myself."

The sassiness of China gives me hope that if as a teacher I nurture the spirit of my students they can soar but that I also have to be willing to catch them when and if they fall. She also taught me the importance of fostering in students an understanding of which battles to fight and which to leave for another day. China possessed an assuredness about herself while at the same time needing reassurance for her feelings from the other women. The two sides of China kept her in trouble with friends, classmates, and professors, but it was the two sides of China that made me treasure her as my student. Always wanting to be the feminist femme fatale China asserted that in the struggle toward justice she wanted to "get there with a little bit of style and a little bit of class." But she knew that the road to equality wasn't going to be easy. In the China way, she said, "It's getting difficult to do my makeup. . . it's a chore to put my lipstick on it's not even fun because my mind is not with it."

Veronica struggled with developing a sense of self. Although she was mature beyond her years she also questioned everything about who she was.

Perhaps it was that maturity that forced her to constantly analyze life. I can still see her at sista dialogue curled up on the sofa listening, arguing, laughing, crying, and questioning. She was committed to finding out about herself, to helping her mother, her friends. She had given herself the duty of bringing other Black women to the place where she now found herself. But Veronica also knew that she had to find the way to taking care of who she was and wanted to be. She understood the negative depictions of Black femaleness and how those depictions had constructed her mother and was determined that the cycle stop with her. Veronica taught me that there were times when I needed to step back and give students a safe space to talk. Silenced in so many ways by so many people students need to experience the liberating effect of just talking and sharing and arriving at a mental place of their design. As a teacher I can and should create that safe space and I can act as a guide on their journey but ultimately the journey is theirs.

A Pedagogy of Wholeness:
Part One—The Theory

Trying to write beyond the assignment of language to a medium of personal expression. I have been cognizant that writing does not translate a reality outside itself but, more precisely, allows the emergence of a new reality. (Simon, 1992, p. 4)

OSHUN: Rochelle, who will help our children? Can you? Will you?

ROCHELLE: Let me tell you a story about Jake. About a year ago I awoke early to put the finishing touches on an article I was completing. It was 5:00 a.m. and I felt relaxed. I knew what was needed to tie all of the disparate pieces together and time, for once, was on my side. I made a fresh pot of coffee and sat to read the paper before I returned to the computer. I vividly remember the instant I sat down with my coffee and looked at the first page of the morning paper my relaxation left me. I was forced to remember why I chose the topic I did, why I had so much trouble theorizing about education, why I got "emotional" whenever I thought about/discussed the miseducation of African American youth.

Staring at me from the front page of *USA Today* was Jake Williams (Johnson, 1997). He appeared to be a handsome Black man. Chocolate complexion, like the sweet-bitter coffee I was drinking, oval eyes that were staring right through me, broad nose that reminded me of the Black men in my life, sensuous lips that seemed to be in a grimace, like only they know the funny and strange secret held by Jake and if the rest of the world knew it they would also smile. As soon as I recorded the picture in my sensory register my brain and heart stepped in and told me Jake was either in trouble or an athlete/entertainer.

OSHUN: I would be willing to bet it was trouble.

ROCHELLE: And you would win. The caption under his picture read, "New prisons isolate worst inmates" and the prison was in Texas, the state that was the last to release enslaved Africans.

OSHUN: So I see they are still trying to hold us.

ROCHELLE: In mind, body, and spirit. I read the story which was filled with words/phrases like "animals," "superbad people," "inhuman," "no hope of parole." There were two smaller pictures on the next page of the article, both of Black men—Curtis Hayden and David Hawkins. Jake, Curtis, David, and all of the unnamed, unpictured Black boys/men and girls/women are why I become angry. My anger hides my fear, showing itself when I am confronted with (as I am daily) the realities of what my young brothers and sisters are experiencing daily.

OSHUN: I know the pursuit of education for African American peoples is not simply academic; it is both a survival and personal pursuit. But I feel a struggle within you, a confusion.

ROCHELLE: I keep asking myself what does Jake have to do with the theme of this book, Black women, and theorizing away the pain. But it is all so connected. I am a Black woman and a teacher, a Black woman who teaches, a Black woman teacher, and my concern does not concentrate itself in one area, with one gender, ignoring the realities of another part of me. The sociopolitical realities of African Americans and all minorities engender pain. The economic realities of African Americans engender pain. If I can effectively help myself and my Black female students theorize away the pain that dominant structures have made synonymous with being Black, then that knowledge is also valuable to all students. I see an attack on African Americans from all sides and especially the far right, which

> VERONICA: Then you got these people who I grew up with in the streets all the time so they don't have an outlet to go to. I know plenty of brothers who "Hey this is where I'm gonna live, average age is thirty say let me make bank now, have a couple of kids by a couple of different women. That's my life.". . . so you figure that is a good majority of urban youth. I remember being a little kid and feeling as though I'm kinda just hangin' in the midst of all this chaos I'm just in there, nothing ever really pertained to me. . . . So you gotta remember when generation X was children. It still was not that many of us on television. I don't remember too many Blacks on TV. Nobody came to us to ask about our self-esteem and how we felt about who we were, their doing that now which I think is lovely but they did not do that with us which is hard because now we are not doing that for our kids. . .
>
> I was the most privileged child in my ghetto neighborhood. "Your mom fix you breakfast every morning." My mom was bacon, eggs, grits, sausage, home fries, the whole nine. What you mean baloney? I had to get with the baloney the cheese and all that. Because even though we lived in the environment my mom did what she could for me, everybody didn't have that. So you figure these are the kids that we are now talking about that are in our generation that have been brought up. I would say the ones with good homes do not nowhere near outweigh the ones. . . I give many props to the girls and guys who made it despite their circumstances 'cause I always say I was in the best circumstances I could have been in my situation and I'm still just coming into mine, still just getting it. . . .
> Sista Dialogue 3/20/99

are providing a framework of domination against African Americans. I need to operate within a Black "way of knowing," which draws a connection between learned knowledge and actual experience, either personal experience or that of the community in general. Jake is both my personal experience and the experience of my community. What happened to Jake is the manifestation of an ideology of modernist thought and action. I had to re-remember Jake to re-remember my reason and purpose for being.

OSHUN: Just keep thinking your way into an understanding. When we accept that this society cares little for its *other* we see it as only logical that they are putting the Jake's of society in a super maximum facility. And it is this same ideology of dehumanization of the *other* that constructs images of Black women. When we see Jake dehumanized and despiritualized we also know that there are countless other Black men and women who are struggling to remain human and whole.

ROCHELLE: The reality of Jake becomes fragmented; thereby mystifying the relationship between the sociopolitical and economic forces, which created the conditions that led to Jake's imprisonment. We understand that the same ideology that constructs superprisons is the ideology that controlled Jake the African American man, forcing him into prison. His guilt or innocence is not as important as what led him to commit a crime or what led the "powers of law enforcement" to accuse him of committing a crime.

Once he entered the superprison, Jake was removed from existence both in the concrete and in the abstract. We, society, are made to forget about the circumstances of Jake's life, the powers that shaped all that Jake is. He is expurgated from and discussed in terms of separation from the social context that defined him. We begin to think that Jake controlled the decisions he made and therefore deserves his punishment for making the wrong decisions. We forget, or are unaware, when we do not look at the social context of Jake's life—that he went to a bad school, had teachers who did not care, could not find a job or found a job beneath his skill level, or had no skills because of a bad school. We forget that Jake saw the front pages of any newspaper and saw African Americans doing wrong. Jake looked at television and saw the "chains and images of psychological slavery" (Akbar, 1989, p. 2). Na'im Akbar states,

> . . . [When slavery] captures the mind and incarcerates the motivation, perception, aspiration, and identity in a web of anti-self images, generating a personal and collective self-destruction, is more cruel than the shackles on the wrist and ankles. The slavery that feeds on the psychology, invading the soul of the man, destroying his loyalties to himself and establishing loyalties to forces which destroy him, is an even worse form of capture. The influences that permit an illusion of freedom, liberation, and self-determination, while tenaciously holding one's mind in subjugation, is the folly of only the sadistic. (p. 2)

Jake could be put in a superprison because the mind that developed the concept of superprison is sadistic. They are certain that Jake is not worth saving, both because of his crime and because of his color. Or maybe his crime is his color.

OSHUN: Rochelle, I know it is hard for you not to feel pain. Remember society is no longer worried about saving Jake; he is unsalvageable. The time and money that could be used to help Jake either before he went to prison or once he was in prison can be better spent ensuring his contact with real humans is limited. It is easier to lock Jake's body away than to reconstruct society into one, that affords liberation, freedom, and equity to all members instead of oppression, objectification, and colonialization to select members.

ROCHELLE: But when I discuss and analyze Jake am I taking away his culpability in the making of his own reality?

OSHUN: No, I think we both accept that Jake made some bad choices and in certain ways created his situation. But at the same time I know that we live in a society, that has historically set up barriers for Black folk. A modernist paradigm seeks to master nature (Kincheloe & Steinberg, 1997). Black men and women represent nature, the object that must be controlled either through force, acquisition, colonization, ideology, culture, on and on and on. The ultimate control for the uncontrollable (animal) is to not only take away every semblance of their humanity and dignity, but also do it in such a way that they have no will to fight. The superprison that encased Jake's body is a metaphor for the prison that tries to encase the souls of our children.

ROCHELLE: I know I get tired of constantly fighting. Despite my exhaustion at least I know how to fight and importantly who to fight against. For Jake control ensures the tools with which to fight have been taken away, or never provided. Although these tools are many and the tool bag is large all are necessary. Political astuteness and power, economic basis, sociological understanding, knowledge of history, etc., come together in an interlocking pattern to weave a relationship of knowing, understanding, and acting on modernist ideology. Since I am a teacher I see education as the dominant pattern that encircles all others.

OSHUN: Did the article say anything about Jakes schooling?

ROCHELLE: No it didn't, but African Americans in educational systems throughout America are experiencing the same devastation. Looking through the lens of education I can place Jake back into the social context of his existence which modernism took him from. It is readily seen that African American education is in a crisis throughout America. From New York to California statistics on educational achievement and disparity between Black and White students fill the pages of national and local reports on schooling for African Americans (Asante, 1991; Fordham, 1988; Gordon, Plana & Keleher, 2000; Jordan-Irving, 1990; Shujja, 1994).

As a society or individual we can make one of two generalizations. First, we could surmise that the evidence of poor school achievement proves (once again) that Black students are incapable of learning and therefore deserve their failure. Moreover, because Black students are incapable of real learning we, as Americans, need not worry about providing educational support in the form of better schools or more effective educational programs.

In contrast, the second option assumes that society in general, as well as the school system, is failing Black students. Although we do not look at Black students as completely victimized objects we nevertheless accept that Black students partake in a colonial educational system that ensures their failure. Joan Davis Ratteray (1991) states:

> Public education wasn't designed for students of color, especially it wasn't designed for African American youngsters. It was designed to develop a consensus, a social contract where the plight of African American children has never been on top of the agenda. Some children are going to make it anyway, but that's a few. The majority of our African American youngsters have to be in a setting that's going to cater to their needs. (p. 103)

OSHUN: And of the two which do you choose?

ROCHELLE: I choose to believe the second option and with this choice comes the responsibility (self- and community-imposed) to *do* something about the situation of African American youth in America's public schools. The emotion I feel every time I read and hear about a Jake can never remain on a purely theoretical plane. I can never "prove" my feelings empirically. I don't have to. Because I name my reality and that of my fellow African American brothers and sisters I am forced to transform the world (Freire, 1970). I have given voice to the problems of Jake and therefore have opened the problems to be renamed.

OSHUN: The power of definition moves Jake from object to subject. You can begin to understand Jake when you place a name on his reality.

ROCHELLE: I like the phrase Freire uses—"Men are not built in silence, but in word, in work, in action-reflection" (1970, p. 76). I also like the term conscientizacao—being conscious of my consciousness. It *names* the pabulum I feast on in acting against the oppressive elements of society that put Jake in a superprison.

OSHUN: But in reality Jake is the reason for a curriculum which provides struggle and survival for Black students. Jake and the thousands (millions?) of children like him are the reason you are here, sitting up at 3:00 a.m. writing and thinking and hoping to make a difference. You see the world and education through Jake. Although you are both Black, he was not able to handle and surpass the suffering brought on by his complexion. You cannot be dispassionate about Jake or analytical regarding what you should and must do.

ROCHELLE: I read and experienced that racism works at the decomposition of the cultural integrity of Blackness (Murrell, 1997). At times I can deal with that and other times I can't find the strength. Thank goodness somewhere in my life I was taught what was needed to get through. In my arsenal of Black survival weapons, I at least had a few, that I could use. But see those things have become so *emic* to my being, so much a part of the total makeup of Rochelle I can no longer name them, identify them. What has been taught to me so that I remain whole and in turn what do I teach my students so they become complete beings?

OSHUN: To answer, or begin to answer, both of your questions we need to remember that U.S. schools are not set up for our success. Of course all of the statistics say that Black students are failing. But more important than that knowledge is to understand the "how" of what is going on.

ROCHELLE: What I am working through and coming to understand is that education, curriculum, pedagogy, theory has to bring about a transformation of Black students into critical cultural agents of change and revolution. Education for Black students cannot afford to be benign. Instead, through education these students must realize how the system is set up for their failure. Subverting it is of the utmost importance.

OSHUN: I should get a T-shirt made that says—*Subverting the Constructs of Education*. Explain education for African Americans, but be brief.

ROCHELLE: To place Black students in a contextual framework, it is vital to consider the root philosophies and goals of the American education system because it is here that African American students struggle to survive. The American educational system performs three essential functions. It both provides information to students and functions as a means of social control. Importantly, schooling is structured as a socialization agency through which the dominant political, social, economic, and cultural norms are imposed and reenforced. As political instruments, schools mold future citizens, maintain and stabilize the political system, and preserve the current balance of political power (Bowles & Gintis, 1976; Nelson, Palonsky & Carlson, 2000; Watkins, 2001). The goals of public education are intrinsically linked to social, political, and economic stability (Spring, 1991). The combination of these functions or goals predetermines what is taught, how it is taught, and who gets taught what.

OSHUN: False knowledge and/or partial knowledge is forced on Black children thereby never allowing them to really understand the realities of being Black in America.

ROCHELLE: Case in point. It was not until 1991 when I started my undergraduate degree that I began to learn Black history. Remember I was 34 when I did my undergrad. It was at that time that I finally had the knowledge to understand the craziness of my parents was in part due to the crap they went through growing up in Alabama in the early 1900s. Pieces of my life or their life finally made sense.

OSHUN: And because you didn't have the information in your cognitive bank it was virtually impossible to truly understand them.

ROCHELLE: Once I gained certain knowledge, even though a part of me was still angry with them, I at least was able to rationalize that anger; it lost its impotency.

OSHUN: Clearly, for African American students, the American education system has not provided access to equality, let alone the *American Dream*.

ROCHELLE: The American Dream for many has been the American Nightmare. The knowledge, culture, and experience of African American students are denigrated or silenced in the public schools while those of the dominant are imposed. Likewise, short- and long-term African American goals (for example, social and economic

> ROCHELLE: How do you understand being Black?
>
> GRACE: I don't know because you see so many things on tv, media, books, in class and each time you have to reevaluate and say is that me? Is that Black? I'm me and yes I'm Black but I don't go with whatever Black is so what and I ain't. . . When I was in private school and we went to a public school and people say I talked white and I dressed white because I dressed really, really nice but hey that hurt too. Hey I'm Black and will always be Black. It's me because I can't say she's Black and I'm like her because there are Black people I am not like. I think that's what I got trapped into and a lot of people get tracked into because you see what is on tv you are not supposed to go here, you are not supposed to talk or act a certain way because you are Black but if I want to talk this way then that's who I am and it doesn't have anything to do with me being Black.
>
> *Sista Dialogue 3/20/99*

equality, and political voice) are undermined in favor of maintaining the status quo. The "dehumanization and despiritualization," which were so much a part of what happened to Jake, is a "truth" for many Black students. Our children are not failing; they are succeeding based on the structures and systems of American society. Since public education was not designed for the achievement of Black children. . .

OSHUN: . . . it therefore attempts to ensure their failure.

ROCHELLE: And although Black and White children enter school on the same level for Black children the longer they stay in school the farther behind they fall (Jordan-Irving, 1990). This holds true in the middle class as much as it does in the lower class. Something depresses Black children at every level of preparation, even the highest. The women in sista dialogue spoke on this point from a personal place. Like Claude Steele (1992), they talked about the devaluation they experienced in the school setting. Throughout schooling, Black students have the added fear that others will see their "full humanity fall with a poor answer or a mistaken stroke of the pen" (Jordan-Irving, 1990,

p. 74). The students have the burden of constantly having to prove themselves. Furthermore, with each new class and level of schooling the acceptance must be won again. The struggle for Black students to gain acceptance is continuous throughout their schooling. They learn that if acceptance is won, it will be hard-won.

OSHUN: The negative images of Black America that you so passionately wrote about in previous chapters are pervasive—they permeate all sectors of American life. What Black youth are exposed to in the television media, newspapers, magazines, and in the lesson plans of the school they attend usually portray African Americans in a negative light. These images are often not even perceived on a conscious level. Over time, however, they are internalized. Blackness is equated with badness. Conversely, Whiteness is equated with goodness and is held up for all to emulate—acting good is equated with acting White. Black children learn to hate who they are. They learn that just as White equals good, Black equals bad. They are disempowered and one of the results is academic underachievement.

ROCHELLE: I guess my writing is passionate because writing helps me process what I am attempting to understand. I didn't enter our conversation knowing the answers for Jake, but when I leave I will have answers.

OSHUN: And additional questions.

ROCHELLE: Yes, but questions that have a purpose. Scanning the newspapers on any given day illuminates the obstacles that face Black people and other ethnic minorities. Poor housing, unequal political representation, high unemployment, lack of Black men and women in positions of power are among the myriad of obstacles that Black children know they must overcome.

OSHUN: What impact does this have on the aspirations of Black children?

ROCHELLE: It creates a contradiction, or ambivalence, in their attitude toward education and their educational achievements. A body of scholars believe that the "main" deterrent to achievement for African American students is caused by the cultural dissonance between public education and the culture of Black children (Boykin,

CAROLE: I'm the only person of color in my class and I just feel like it's my job to like open their eyes and to like, its just like, I love the class and it's good discussion and they are open enough to listen to what I am, to what I have to say, but I'm the one who always has to talk up and it just makes me so tired and I'm thinking, I'm not even graduated yet. I'm not even out there confronting principals and school boards and parents, you know, and other teachers, and I'm like these are the people I'm going to be working with and they already have this preconceived idea? So, in one aspect, on one hand, it makes me frustrated by their words and tired, but then on the other hand, sometimes I'm like, if I'm not gonna do it Who will? You know, and I'm like, I have to, I mean all those little kids that were like looking up at me with those big eyes, they need someone to pave the way for them. You see how much problems there are and so

2000; Jagers & Carroll, 2002; Jordan-Irving, 1990). According to the cultural difference framework the failure of African American students in the public school system is a direct result of the incompatibility of the dominant curriculum and African American norms.

Children from non-European, lower socioeconomic status cultural groups are at a disadvantage in the school because the American educational system has evolved out of a European philosophical, theoretical, and pedagogical context. White children are involved in an educational experience that complements their culture, whereas Black children exist within an educational system that denies Black culture. Not only does the educational system deny Black culture it also denies Black children having talent beyond athletics. This denial is a primary reason for the academic underachievement of Black students. Janice Hale-Benson (1986) agrees that the difficulties Black children's experience in school have their antecedents in the fact that the educational system exists under a "different culture than their own" (p. 84). She stresses the importance of laying the foundation for delineating and identifying those points of mismatch between Black culture and European American culture that may have educational consequences for Black children.

> you can either become tired—and we are allowed to be tired once in a while because if you don't just take a break from it then we're gonna crumple ourselves, but I think it's good to see how much problems there are out there, it's also inspiration to go out and try to do something about it.
>
> STACY: Maybe in your class you should bring up the next time the diversity issue comes up, be like why is it that I'm the only one that can talk about this? How come nobody else addresses Black students or maybe this trouble that little Black children or minority children may have in a White classroom I guess, if that's what your class is about. These are the people you have to deal with and you can't treat everyone the same because not everybody is the same. . .so maybe they'll see that, "Maybe you really are ignorant if that crosses your mind as a teacher" that I'm going to have a child who's Hispanic in an all-white school or something like that and the different things that they need. If you're supposed to be the teacher, you're supposed to be the educators, why don't you educate yourself first?
>
> *Sista Dialogue 3/20/1999*

OSHUN: Are you placing cultures in a hierarchal relationship?

ROCHELLE: The treatment of cultural difference does not imply that one culture is superior to the other. What it does is recognize the importance of cultural differences in pedagogical practices. Jordan-Irving (1990) notes that even in instances where non-Black teachers acknowledge the cultural differences it may result in further racial stereotyping, differential treatment, and lower teacher expectations when they are unfamiliar with Black culture.

OSHUN: Hold on. You are creating a binary between Black and White teachers and placing each within some hierarchy of understanding the essence of Blackness.

ROCHELLE: Shit, I guess I did. Let me rephrase what I just said. I realize that there can be good and dedicated White teachers and poor and clueless Black teachers. What I meant to say was that regardless of the "color" of the teacher, if they do not practice a culturally relevant pedagogy, then they are creating an environment that makes learning difficult.

OSHUN: Okay that statement is a little better but you need to watch yourself in the future.

ROCHELLE: Well, regardless of the connection between the cultural incongruity of Black children and school, it appears relevant for minority student success. Because the culture of Black children is often ignored, misunderstood, or discounted, Black children will often experience cultural discontinuity in school. The combination of Afrocentric students and Eurocentric schools results in conflict because of a lack of cultural congruence (Jordan-Irving, 1990). This lack of cultural synchronization becomes evident in instructional situations in which teachers misinterpret, devalue, and dismiss Black students' language, nonverbal cues, physical movements, learning styles, cognitive approaches, and worldview. When teachers and students are out of synchronization, they "clash and confront each other, both consciously and unconsciously in matters concerning proxemics, the use of interpersonal distance; paralanguage, the behaviors accompanying speech, such as voice tone, pitch, speech rate, and length; and coverbal behavior, gesture, facial expression, eye gaze" (Jordan-Irving, 1990, p. xxi).

Black student empowerment and Black revolutionary thought are two dynamics that are complementary. The dynamics between the two make it possible for the world not to be someplace where we must be tolerated or that we want or have to find some quiet corner and hide away. Instead, we look at the world as something, given the right tools, we can change. Empowerment is agency. Agency is the ability to act on and change our world/environment. We must remember that while we want and strive for individual empowerment, only collective action can effectively generate lasting social transformation of political and economic institutions.

In order to reach educational parity for Black children, an educational system must recognize and integrate Black culture into the school. Clearly cultural difference negatively affects Black students, thereby causing or exacerbating underachievement. The importance of a culturally relevant curriculum and pedagogy in the academic achievement of minority students has been a prevalent theory among African American scholars (Henry, 1994; Lee, Lomety, & Shujjaa, 1990; Lomotey, 1991; Steele, 1992).

OSHUN: Okay, I understand the importance of culturally relevant curriculum for Black students. But tell me how you are using it to develop a pedagogy to theorize away the pain of Black women? Better yet, how is it helping you to understand Jake?

ROCHELLE: I am seeking greater understanding through Jake and the impact a racist society had on him. He is the foundation to my ruminations. And as the foundation I place the various theories of African American education on him to see if they afford me a greater understanding of what put his picture on the front page of *USA Today*. Clearly African American children must receive something other than what they are getting in our educational system. An effective reform of education and schooling must be concerned with all areas of a Black child's existence.

OSHUN: Existence? To me that sounds like what education is already doing—allowing us to merely exist, nothing more.

ROCHELLE: You're right. Instead of existence lets say transformation. To transform means that I don't just look at what happens in school but I attempt to understand everything that constructs a Black child's reality and then I plan accordingly. As such I can develop an educational theory, which deconstructs and then allows students to reconstruct who they are, individually and collectively. My purpose is to define and construct what is needed in a pedagogy, which reconceptualizes the realities of Black students. I have positioned myself in such a way that I am forced to accept that there are many difficult societal barriers to the self of Jake. But that understanding also tells me that ultimately as a teacher, and someone who works at teacher reform, education can and must provide to Black students a belief in self.

A Pedagogy of Wholeness

OSHUN: Let's return to your earlier question of what we teach students so that they become complete beings.

ROCHELLE: Schooling—as it is theorized and practiced—despiritualizes and dehumanizes Black children, or at the very least it does nothing to return what society has taken away (King, 1994). Black children enter the educational system and begin to lose their concept of self from the very first day they sit in class ignored by the curriculum, the teacher, and the system. Bit by bit, they are stripped of the seed of humanity that is part of their ontological makeup. As they grow and mature into adulthood the struggle to regain what school and society robbed from them begins to eat away, causing anger. It's like a cancer that invades the body, destroying the inside as well as the outside.

OSHUN: Moraga, the deep sister that she is, asked, "How do we organize ourselves to survive this war? To keep our families, our bodies, our spirits intact?"

ROCHELLE: There is a war I too wonder about as I struggle to hold onto the pieces of my spirit that are under assault. Moraga and Anzuldula (1981), tell us that:

Sometimes in the face of my own/our own limitations, in the face of such worldwide suffering, I doubt even the significance of books. Surely this is the same predicament so many people who have tried to use words as weapons have found themselves in—*?Cara a cara con el enemigo de qúe valen mis palabras?* Face to face with enemy, what good are my words? (Npn)

OSHUN: What good are words if they are from the language of the oppressor?—none. What we must instead do is develop a language of critique, but one in our own voice filled with anger, emotion, and caring. "Ultimately the liberation of our thought from its colonized condition will require the creation of a new language" (Ani, 1994, p .10).

ROCHELLE: If not careful words can be limiting or a weapon against us. Instead, we develop our own language—one filled with truth, honesty, anger, emotion, spiritualness, pride—to critique the war waged against us. We are in a war for the souls of our children and my goal as an educator is to foster a critical consciousness in my students. As such I try to create a way of interacting, which brings students to a Black consciousness.

OSHUN: And a pedagogy of wholeness works at creating this language of critique? So how does it differ from the various pedagogical sites, which are already out there in the educational realm?

ROCHELLE: I believe that education should work at the whole person. When education targets wholeness of being and spirituality, individual and collective transformation happens. A transformative pedagogy has two distinct and related parts. First, a sociopolitical transformation must occur for the student, which allows the second part, life transformation, to happen. When I use critical pedagogy, students realize their connection to the world. They begin to understand the political and economic structures of domination and oppression and develop tools for change. And this is something I would bet Jake didn't experience in his schooling.

OSHUN: Critical pedagogy is the framing tool that provides a language of critique to question the structures of the education system in general and classroom pedagogy in particular. According to Giroux and Simon (1989), critical pedagogy

> refers to a deliberate attempt to influence how and what knowledge and identities are produced within and among particular sets of social relations. It can be understood as a practice through which people are incited to acquire a particular "moral character." As both a political and practical activity, it attempts to influence the occurrence and qualities of experiences. (p. 239)

Critical pedagogy can/should be transformative. I don't have patience with a teacher who professes to use critical pedagogy but doesn't want to deal with transformative thinking.

ROCHELLE: When I use Jake as the foundation to my understanding, it is clear that to effectively educate Black children a pedagogy must frame schooling and teaching within a critical dynamic that affords students an ability to name their world, to reflect critically on self and society, and have the agency to act for change (Giroux, 1997; Kincheloe, 2004; McLaren, 2000; Pozo, 2003; Wink, 1997). This ability changes the student from an object to be constructed to a subject in the construction of their own knowledge. As such, critical pedagogy speaks to issues of power, how power is distributed to some and kept from others and what influence it has on schooling. Critical pedagogy forces the student and teacher to view the world critically, taking nothing for granted but instead questioning the reasons behind various systems of domination.

Two important tools Black children need, which critical pedagogy offers, are the ability to read the word and read the world. When Black children read the word they can decode and encode those words by understanding the words as they relate to their experiences, possibilities, culture, and knowledge. And I know just like I know that I am Black, that if Jake had that tool then he could have understood negative depictions in text surrounding Blackness. Rather than accepting and internalizing as truth he would be able to place the negativity in context. Not dismiss it but understand the purposes dominant structures in society had in putting it out there. He would know the workings of hegemony.

OSHUN: I feel a problem with critical pedagogy. Are you too accepting of its "power"?

ROCHELLE : No. I understand that despite its obvious benefits it stops short of being a revolutionary force in the education of Black students. Critical pedagogy is often more concerned with the individual and their ability to critique and change their world whereas culturally relevant pedagogy concerns itself with collective action and is "grounded in cultural understandings, experiences, and ways of knowing the world" (Ladson-Billings, 1992, pp. 382–383). In her critique of critical pedagogy, Ellsworth (1992) asserts that "the goal of critical pedagogy was a critical democracy, individual freedom, social justice, and social change—a revitalized public sphere characterized by citizens capable of confronting public issues critically through ongoing forms of public debate and social action" (p. 302). She continues by saying that the language of critical pedagogy operates at a "high level of abstraction" (p. 302) offering "decontextualized criteria for choosing one position over others" (p. 303). Accordingly, the abstraction that some attribute to critical pedagogy serves to alienate its concepts from the very people it aims to help.

OSHUN: I agree. Much of what I read through your eyes discussed critical pedagogy in language that can be so inaccessible it turns folks off. Another question or problem I have with critical pedagogy is that the place of minorities is not central in its framing. I don't see us.

ROCHELLE: Which is why we, I, must take the "bits and pieces" from various other theories to create what I need. For me the term "pedagogy of wholeness" underscores the varied inadequacies of other pedagogies. It is hard as hell being Black in America and one of anything ain't gone get it. Because of that I take whatever little pieces of various pedagogies to create my own. Critical, cultural, transformative, Afrocentric, feminist, etc. For example, when we layer Afrocentric theory onto critical pedagogy we can challenge the structures of oppression in society and call for change. The problematics and hegemony of critical pedagogy utilize the voices of mostly White male scholars, giving legitimacy to their work; on the other hand, Afrocentric theory uses Black scholars in understanding Black realities. Afrocentric theory is distinct and in ways opposed to a Eurocentric worldview (Asante, 1991; Asante & Atwater, 1986). Traditional scholarship defines the worldview of Black people as "reflections of quantifiable, biological differences among humans or residual categories that emerged in response to institutionalized racism" (Collins, 1991, p. 27). In contrast, Afrocentric theory states that an Afrocentric belief system reflects a "longstanding belief system among African people" and that "being Black encompasses both experiencing White domination and individual and group valuation of an independent, long-standing Afrocentric consciousness" (Collins, 1991, p. 27).

Framing a pedagogy through the lens of Afrocentric theory allows Black students to be central to its development. What happens when Black children are placed at the center of a pedagogy? Lee, Lomotey, and Shujja (1990) contend that an African-centered pedagogy has the following goals:

1. legitimizes African stores of knowledge;
2. positively exploits and scaffolds productive community and cultural practices;
3. extends and builds on the indigenous language;
4. reinforces community ties and idealizes service to one's family, community, nation, race, and world;
5. promotes positive social relationship;
6. imparts a worldview that idealizes a positive, self-sufficient future for one's people without denying the self-worth and right to self-determination of others; and
7. supports cultural continuity while promoting critical consciousness (p. 50).

OSHUN: Henry (1994) states that an African-centered pedagogy resists dominant structures that "damage Black children's spirits and self-identity" (p. 300). Yet despite the positive influences of an African-centered pedagogy, gender bias is often inherent in Afrocentric scholarship.

ROCHELLE: Which is why I need to utilize a Black womanist theory in my little mixture of understanding. Black feminist thought utilizes a structural analysis of the intersection of race, class, and gender when theorizing a Black woman's standpoint. This becomes an epistemological discussion of not only who creates knowledge but how knowledge is created.

I have discussed Black feminist thought throughout this book. I have talked about its epistemology, its understanding of various types of knowledge. I have stated that Black feminist thought is not only concerned with the intersection of race, class, and gender but also the interface of politics, history, the economy, and society.

When I think of Jake and the Black women I teach, I clearly see that growing in a critical way would allow all the ability to read the world. For Jake, his surroundings—peoples, places, and things—would have lost (much of) their mystification and therefore their power. See, it's all about life transformation. Afrocentric theory in education does that, in part. Students stop thinking of themselves in individualistic terms and instead as part of a community, realizing their freedom cannot come at the expense of the freedom of all Black people. Students understand the historical connections between struggle and survival and they create a self-defined standpoint.

OSHUN: Can I call it a revolution of the mind and soul?

ROCHELLE: I like the sound of that. As we try to demystify Jake's world, (the visible and invisible), a mental revolution will be the vehicle. And when we move a step past critical pedagogy we create a revolutionary force. Remember earlier I said that I see and analyze my world through the lens of education. The way I see it is that education must provide the intellectual catalyst towards both revolutionary thought and action.

OSHUN: Thought and action for whom? Articulate what you mean.

ROCHELLE: It would provide thought and action for self first and then extend it to the Black community. As I think about the pedagogies and theories out there I need to see that they foster, promote, and teach for revolution. Culturally relevant pedagogy urges *collective* action grounded in cultural understandings, experiences, and ways of knowing the world versus the more individualistic nature of critical pedagogy (Ladson-Billings, 1992). But don't think that I am completely dismissing critical pedagogy. It has its place in creating a public space populated by politically empowered people who are knowledgeable about how to shape the political and social agenda to critical democracy, individual freedom, social justice, and social change (Ellsworth, 1992).

OSHUN. So what you are saying is that if we take the benefits of these various pedagogical sites, then a fuller pedagogy is born.

ROCHELLE: I have been attempting to develop a purpose for an Afriwomanist pedagogy of wholeness within a variety of pedagogical sites. I find myself still thinking through questions of pedagogy given certain types of epistemological concerns. By combining critical pedagogy, Afrocentric theory, and Black feminist thought I can engage in the dialectics of micro-level and macro-level structures that are working to oppress Black women. I hope to stretch critical pedagogy by looking at the three theories that speak to me. The goal of theory is to have a description and sense of the world which allows me to write and teach about Black women.

OSHUN: As you understand it so far, what is a pedagogy of wholeness? How is it theorized and practiced? Who really needs it? How does it differ from the various pedagogical sites which are already out there in the educational realm?

ROCHELLE: My pedagogy must foster in Black students the knowledge of self—being in touch with the world as a Black person. King (1994) tells us that "Being free is based on knowing one's humanity from within" (p. 270). Vanzant (1995) reminds us that "Spirituality examines and reveals the truth of your being" (p. 189). She adds, "Everything happens twice, first on the inside and then on the outside" (p. 201). That is why I need to combine the three theories to create a wholeness in my pedagogy. What I feel is essential to Black students is the complete whole, the closure to the circle of existence. I want to work on the mind but I need to work on the spirit as well.

OSHUN: We can never forget to work with the spirit of a child. Recognizing the importance of the spirit "An African centered critical pedagogy resists the dominant structures, which damage Black children's spirits and self-identity" (Henry, 1994, p. 300).

ROCHELLE: I have come to believe that working on the spirit of the individual must come before they will even accept or think important the socio-political information I want to impart. When in your heart you believe you are nothing you can memorize the facts in order to pass a test, but the information really does not and cannot transform beyond that. I have had too many Black students who received and could regurgitate the information I provided but the information was not life changing. On the other hand, I have had Black students whom I have watched over the years *become*.

OSHUN: Do you mean become in touch with self, knowing and learning self, in touch with who they are?

ROCHELLE: All of that plus an understanding of the process of rehumanizing self. Of placing self back into the life equation. Of loving all parts of self. "The Valley of Love is designed to teach us that the only relationship we can have in this life is the relationship we are having with ourselves" (Vanzant, 1995, p. 296). When all of this is not present the "best" pedagogy on the bookshelf will mean nothing, because it cannot force the information upon Black students. They have to be ready to accept and internalize what you give. I believe that Jake's "clarity of soul was missing" (King, 1994) allowing the pain to fester in that empty space.

I'm going to backtrack for a moment. I began this process wondering what my pain and the pain of my Black female students had to do with teaching. I realized that my personal pain was allowed because my belief in self had never been fully developed. Because of my arrested development I could feel and experience the negative and the positive, always allowing the negative to win. I vividly recall making Phi Beta Kappa and immediately calling my therapist with the news. At our next visit he said he wondered who was going to walk in his office—the woman who made Phi Beta Kappa or the woman who doubted everything about her intellect. On that day, it was the latter who entered the office; my euphoria had lasted less than a day. I immediately went back to the Rochelle unsure of self.

At the same time I realized the origins of my pain, I realized that for many Black women and Black people the pain originated from the same place inside that was missing something. I can understand Jake because my "clarity of soul" was also missing (King, 1994) and as a Black teacher who cares for the spirit of Black students I knew I had to include my journey towards that clarity in my pedagogy and philosophy of education. Education should be the means toward Black students reestablishing their connection with self and the world (Henry 1993, 1994; King, 1994; Shujja, 1994). Moreover, education should be the key to a student unlocking the mysteries of their existence and provide the road map to creating their own knowledge. For Black women education should not only afford them an understanding of the sociopolitical forces that oppress, but also ensure that the new knowledge is internalized with enough strength to uproot the old.

A vitalness of humanity is essential to the education of Black students and Black women. King (1994) gives a definition of human vitalness as:

> aliveness of the human spirit expressed with honest vigor... being awake; looking; seeing, tasting, and engaging in nonoppressive uses of the power of one's autonomous soul; participating in self's human rights and responsively demonstrating the Afrohumanity of caring, closeness, creating, and calling for truth. (p. 271)

She crafts her language with such love and care for Black thought and existence and at the same time it is solid language, grounded in Black cultural theory; a cultural theory which determines the trajectory of not only our (as Black people) existence but our transformation. The healthy survival of Black women is dependent on the transformative, human vitality education should provide.

OSHUN: Would "clarity of soul" have helped Jake surmount the obstacles in his way?

ROCHELLE: I think so. Wait, I know so. The most important issue to me as a teacher and as a political activist working toward social justice and equity for all students is to foster that belief in self. Okay, go with me on this. Let's say that the story attached to Jake's picture is positive. Let's pretend that his education allowed him to grow into the man his ancestors intended him to be.

OSHUN: How? Does your scenario include creating a different social reality for his life?

ROCHELLE: No, that would be a dream. My scenario, which is based in theory, is about the possibilities if we do what is within our power to do. Unfortunately, I cannot change the destructive society Jake found himself living in. What I'm doing is putting him in an educational system that provides the tools he needed to transform his world.

OSHUN: So how do we meet Jake in this new picture?

ROCHELLE: The same way. I still see Jake's picture on the front page of *USA Today* in an article about Texas and the creation of these maximum-security superprisons. But now Jake's story is not that of an inmate, but of a man fighting to have the money spent in his daughter's school system instead of the prison system. He is not a politician but a concerned parent who understands the workings of the political system. He is astute and politically and socially aware.

Jake's consciousness was created when all around him allowed Blackness to become central to his being. Jake is not lost. Instead he is framed within a Black consciousness and therefore connected to himself and his community. Because Black children were placed at the center, Jake experienced a system that loved and supported his full development.

OSHUN: Damn, that's so true.

ROCHELLE: It is my job—no, my obligation—as a teacher to center the margin, in my own mind, of Black existence. Black folk exist (in the minds of others) at the margins of society. I must destroy that concept, not only in my reality, but also in the reality of my students. I must teach them how to bring their life into the center. As a Black teacher I must teach my students to rebel, fight, learn, struggle, know, believe in themselves—and that belief will then afford a wholeness of spirit. This is the only way I was able to survive and come out able to find wholeness, having a sense of struggle and commitment as a Black person. This is the best way to allow the same for my students. I do it in the spirit of Jake.

Transition

Michael

I have a wonderful poster board filled with memories of my high school students that is placed strategically above my desk. Whenever I become discouraged or start to ask myself what am I doing in graduate school instead of out in the "real" world, working with "real" problems, I look at that board and re-remember the stories that led me to graduate school. I remember the lofty goals I had set for myself as a teacher and I remember my failures and successes in reaching those goals. Most importantly, I remember that my purpose in graduate school is to understand my failures and be able to replicate my successes.

Why did all of my good intentions not always do what I had intended them to do? Why did a school (administration, faculty, and staff) that was intended for an "at-risk" population not care and strive for the success of its students? Why were some of the students "stuck in stupid," insistent upon making decisions that were harmful to them? Why did so many students possess the I-don't-give-a-damn attitude, see no way out, live only for today, disengage from the culture of school, drop out? Why were those in control sitting and letting a portion of society fail?

One of my students represents for me the statistic we constantly read about in educational journals. Michael, a young Black male from the inner city living in a female-headed household, dealing and taking drugs, drinking, dropping in and out of school, hustling, despising authority, was my big failure. Michael was special, and as irritating as he often could be, I somehow managed to place my identity as a good teacher in his hands. If I could affect Michael in a positive way then I could perform wonders for all of the students to come. Despite the burden I placed on Michael, I actually did not have a great deal of classroom time with him because his attendance at school depended upon his attendance in jail. The times he was in class I talked, threatened, and bribed in my attempt to get Michael to work, to see the importance/necessity of school work. I told him he could change his situation; he was smart and had something to offer to the world and to himself. I told him that he had a debt to his community and all of the African Americans who had struggled and died to make sure he had the chances they were denied. I tried to make world history relevant to him and when that didn't work I told him what my momma told me, "You do the work because I said so!" When Michael bothered to show up for class I usually had to play the barter game—you do something for me and I'll do something for you. For example, if Michael sat quietly and read his text for 20 minutes then he could play a computer game or listen to his Walkman. I only kicked Michael out of class once and that was when he was drinking bourbon on the rocks in class. Usually I could handle his tantrums and I always felt if I kicked him out of class he would get into more trouble out on the streets. Of course, there were times when class was running smoothly and I was tired and out of patience and I prayed Michael didn't show up and disrupt the flow—at least not today.

Michael completely rejected the curriculum and schooling. He came to school when he had nothing else to do or when he needed to meet one of his "boys." Michael understood a reality that said a high school education was not going to make any difference in his life. He saw himself as both a victim of society and his color and he lived with its resulting directionless anger. For the generation Michael represents, immediate gratification was a necessity because tomorrow was too far away and too uncertain. Michael was not a case study of social reproduction in action because through his actions he would fall in status much below the achievements of his parents.

Michael is currently in prison for rape and murder. On his way to a crack house Michael stopped to rape and then shoot a female crack addict. What is ironic is the Michael who seldom came to school was in my class for two days after he committed the crime. The Friday before he was arrested I sat with Michael and several other students and had a "rap" session about life. I told Michael that he was wasting his life being high. I argued with him for coming to class "stoned" and told him he was disrespecting himself and me. He told me that when he was high he thought clearly, accused me of trying to be a counselor and then apologized for being disrespectful. We joked about having the munchies, the bell rang for the end of the day and we all said good-bye. The next day another teacher from school called and told me to read the paper. I sat and read the story about Michael and cried for hours. I had lost. The following week I applied to graduate school, determined to find the answers and ask the right questions.

In my second year of graduate school I sat drinking coffee at 5:00 a.m. reading the story of Jake and thinking about Michael. Both of their stories held the same pain and frustration of a life not fulfilled. Both of their stories hurt me deeply as a Black woman. I imagined the two meeting and discussing the similarities of their separate lives. Knowing Michael and imaging Jake brought me to a place where I could touch the knowledge needed to understand and change the world or at least my world.

I knew that there was a connection between Michael and Jake and all of the Black students I had taught in the past and would teach in the future. But I had to ask myself if I had made that connection? Had I allowed my awareness of Michael to expand my conceptual understanding of pedagogy? In the two years that had elapsed between Michael and Jake had I become any wiser? Was my philosophy of teaching different than it had been two years prior?

My answer to those questions was neither yes or no but a combination of the two. In some ways I was wiser because I had been exposed to and accepted for myself new knowledge. More importantly I had learned how to embrace my subjugated knowledge. It's the joining of the new and the subjugated knowledge that on some level has always constructed my identity. But I did not always accept the knowing that was part of me as being real or worthy of respect. Theoretically I understand the binary construction of my knowledge. I understood in the abstract the false split between what books told me and what I knew to be real but still I compartmentalized. There was Jake the unknown and Michael the known and what I understood about each were never joined thereby affording a more complete understanding of both. Instead I needed to learn how to connect the parts of my knowing creating a collage of knowledge. Each separate part stands out, yet they also blend and tell a different story when viewed in their whole.

A Pedagogy of Wholeness:
Part Two—The Practice

OSHUN: Tell me about your classroom. How do you implement an Afriwomanist pedagogy of wholeness in your class?

ROCHELLE: I see, talk to, so many Black women who are struggling to believe in themselves, instead they end up doubting their existence, right to Be. The most important issue to me as a teacher and as a political activist working toward social justice and equity for all students is to bridge that disconnect. My concern, my area of interest is in the curriculum/pedagogy needed for Black and Brown children in schools. What type of education is needed? What type of education will be empowering? How do I as an instructor foster in my students a commitment toward radical agency?

These are a few of the questions I have asked myself and am still struggling to answer. I realize that there are inequalities, poor schools, racist teachers, bad curriculum, children coming into the class ill-prepared to learn. There are countless reform movements aimed at making schools better. Some movements blame the teachers, others blame the students, still others blame the whole concept of schools for what is taking place. And all seem to fail.

Despite the various "failures" in school reform/teaching reform movements we must "keep on pushing" for the sake of Black children. In a discussion on effective teaching, Foster (1994) posits that it was apparent

> the extent to which the teacher's philosophy of teaching and her pedagogy had been influenced by and was grounded in her social and cultural experience in the Black community. (p. 137)

I read, I see, I understand on one level what Foster is discussing but on another level I still wonder what can I take from all I have read and lived to guide my attempt to complete what I have to complete? How can I "dance with theory" in a rhythm, which is indigenous to my culture?

OSHUN: Gestalt—understand all the parts of your whole. As an African American woman in a society that devalues us at every turn, survival is often the main goal. From negative depictions on television to negative depictions in the ideology of America, African American women are under a constant siege, battling for survival. How do you enact the previous 100 pages in your classroom or is this all an exercise in futility?

ROCHELLE: As a critical teacher, I try to force my students to understand the anger and also the pride I feel in my Black womanism. More importantly, I lead them to an understanding of the "culture of survival" that Black women have historically possessed.

In *The African American Woman*, my students and I discuss the insidious ways Black women are constructed in society. We discuss the social, historical, political, and economic realities of Black women. Many of my students enter class thinking it is going to be a history class and they will learn names, achievements, and dates of Black women. Instead, I begin the class with a word list scribbled on one-half of the bulletin board—*ideology, epistemology, deconstruction, hegemony, devaluation, Other, dichotomy, binary opposition, stereotypes*. I then ask the students for adjectives they think of when describing Black women. Of course they begin with politically correct, positive words—*strong, beautiful, mother*—until I tell them to be honest and tell me the words that most of society uses to describe Black women. At that point there is a free for all as students hurl words at me faster than I can write them down—*slut, ho, matriarch, ugly, sexual, aggressive, demanding, fat, unattractive, teen mothers, strong*. Once the board is filled I just let them look at the words, allow the words to seep into their consciousness.

OSHUN: Aren't they, the words, already part of their consciousness?

ROCHELLE: Singularly maybe but not together. It's the impact of students seeing the board dripping with the venom within the words that I'm after.

OSHUN: Kind of the drama queen aren't you?

ROCHELLE: Whatever it takes. It's important that the students realize from the start that this is not a history class and we are not going to go through a long litany of historical facts on Black women. If that is what they are expecting then read a book but don't take this class expecting to get that information. Instead, we are going to analyze the construction of Black womanhood and the etymology of these words through the lenses of ideology, epistemology, the *Other*, deconstruction, hegemony, devaluation, dichotomy, binary opposition, stereotypes. They must learn these concepts, pay close attention to them in their readings, because it is through an understanding of these concepts that they will begin to partially open the door in their realization of Black women. Whatever time remains in the class on that first day is spent talking about the meaning of Black feminist thought—its purposes, goal, and benefit to our understanding of Black women.

Borrowing from Patricia Collins, I divided the discussion of African American women into five themes: Black Feminist Thought, Legacy of Struggle, Representation and Controlling Images, Search for Voice, and

Empowerment in Everyday Life. Through readings, documentaries, films, and class discussions, the class dissects the life of African American women. This dissection allows the students (Black and White, male and female) to understand the various ways ideology has attempted to control and dominate African American women. In addition, an understanding of Black feminist thought allows the students to see the ways Black women are not only deconstructing the race, gender, and class oppression of Black women but also Black female activism and empowerment.

I am aware of the need to assess the abstract through concrete experience. Although I use *Black feminist thought* to teach students the theory that underlies Black women's lives, I also weave in *We Are Your Sisters: Black Women in the Nineteenth Century*, an anthology of Black women's writings edited by Dorothy Sterling (1984). In this excellent volume students read firsthand accounts of Black women under enslavement, freedom, the war, and post-World War I through letters, diaries, interviews, and Freedman Bureau records. In this way two purposes are served: the first is the women become subjects in their own history and are no longer objectified by present-day scholars. Students are allowed to hear their voices, concerns, and intelligence, and then relate that voice to the tenets of Black feminism. For example, they receive a glimpse of the bewilderment and confusion the concept of freedom caused some enslaved people. Take for example the following passage:

> *Member de fust Sunday of freedom. We was all sittin' roun' restin' an' tryin' to think what freedom meant an' ev'ybody was quiet an' peaceful. All at once ole Sister Carrie who was near 'out a hundred started in to talkin':*

> *Tain't no mo' sellin today,*
> *Tain't no mo' hirin' today,*

> *Tain't no pullin off shirts today,*
> *Its stomp down freedom today.*
> *Stomp it down!*

An' when she says "Stomp it down," all de slaves commence to shoutin' wid her:

> *Stomp down freedom today-*
> *Stomp it down!*
> *Stomp down Freedom today.* (Sterling, 1984, p. 244)

OSHUN: You trouble and layer the realities of knowledge or in some cases what we think we know. Speaking of knowledge I remember once how you used the book to lay the guilt trip big-time on your students.

ROCHELLE: As soon as I realized my class was not doing the assigned reading I recited a passage from *We Are Your Sisters* where various women discussed their struggle to learn to read during enslavement, despite fear of death if discovered. I had to bring it home to the students. Personal accountability (Collins, 1991) is not just a notion. In my class I made students accountable for their actions and when they fucked up I let them know.

OSHUN: It's the juxtaposition of accountability within the ethic of caring—both qualities of effective/affective teaching.

ROCHELLE: In addition, students begin to appreciate that African/African American women who happened to be enslaved understood their objectification and oppression at the hands of a cruel system and found ways to survive. Either due to a lack of education or miseducation, many students believe that other than Sojourner Truth and Harriet Tubman, slave women were just singing in the fields and accepting their conditions. Black women have always participated in the legacy of resistance and struggle from the social, historical, and political conditions of society. For example, Lewis Hayden, a leader of Boston's Black community in the 1900s, tells of how his mother kept her children from being sold:

> My mother often hid us all in the woods, to prevent master selling us. When we wanted water, she sought for it in any hole or puddle formed by falling trees or otherwise. It was often full of tadpoles and insects. She strained it, and gave it round to each of us in the hollow of her hand. For food, she gathered berries in the woods, got potatoes, raw corn & c. After a time, the master would send word to her to come in, promising he would not sell us. (Hayden, in Sterling, 1984, p. 58)

It was important for my students to understand the strength that these women possessed despite the hell they were living in. I often reminded them of the words and images we wrote on the board the first day of class so that they could see the dichotomy between the reality of Black women and the perception of Black women.

Although I occasionally use the didactic method when there was particular information the students needed, my pedagogy is built around the second characteristics of an African American epistemology, the use of dialogue in assessing knowledge claims. In the African American community, words carry power. An African American epistemology demands discourse which pursues the connectedness of dialogue (Collins, 1991). Connectedness, an important part of African American roots, asserts that the importance of community outweighs the need of the individual in African American thought which is related to a sense of being human (Asante, 1991; Collins, 1991). Asante (1991) believes that becoming human or realizing the promise of becoming human is the only task of the person. Likewise, Collins (1991) asserts that people become human and empowered only in the context of a community, and only when they "become seekers of the type of connections, interactions, and meetings that lead to harmony" (p. 185).

OSHUN: The community of women that developed in sista dialogue is analogous to that point. The women created this wonderful mixture of speaking in distinct yet collective ways.

ROCHELLE: And that is also what I strive for in my class. I create a safe space where the freedom exists to explain self and others. When a teacher engages a class in personal introspection they must be prepared to hear the painful questioning of students. In one log entry a Black female student cried, "Me questioning me. . . am I the source of the friction never forgetting or forgiving?" (log entry, 7/10/97). She went on to say,

> I started to question the fact if there was racism, because the people in that circle would never express or better yet *have* or *entertain* an ill thought against a black person. . . BULLSHIT! I *know* that when I have Jamier people look at us strange. I *know* that when I am with a white guy people stare! I *know* that my colored skin matters! I *know* when people see me some tell me I'M pretty for a Black girl. I *know* when I talk to people about State they assume I'm here on scholarship or because of affirmative action. I *know* that people give me grief because I am an African-American. I *know* that I was scared for my boyfriend every time he drove home. I *know* that I *know*. Being in that class made me wonder. Made me wonder about reasoning and logic. (log entry, 7/10/97)

OSHUN: Do you think you make learning meaningful for your students?

ROCHELLE: I believe that to make learning a meaningful experience students must become active in the attainment of knowledge. In order for this to happen, it is critical to create a space within the class in which student–teacher and student–student discourse can occur. For this reason, at least 70% of class time is spent in discussion, where we critically analyze the class readings in a sociohistorical context. Each semester many students enter the class afraid to speak, fearful that their knowledge will not be valued or they will have nothing important to add to the discussion. Students of all colors and classes, though to different degrees, have been silenced through years of schooling in a system that operates on the belief that noncredentialed knowledge is unimportant. Although at first apprehensive to speak, eventually most students begin to use their voice and engage in dialogue where they are using their specialized knowledge to theorize about the taken-for-granted or personal feelings and experiences they hold.

One of my greatest challenges is that if I become too theoretical I lose sight of the subjugated knowledge, which has helped Black people survive in this country since the 1600s. Finding a method to combine my empirical and experiential way of knowing is paramount to my survival both as a teacher and a Black woman. More importantly, it is paramount that I use my personal dilemma to appreciate the realities of students and better equip my pedagogical philosophy to foster a mental/spiritual decolonization of the mind and spirit.

OSHUN: Simon (1992) states, "Trying to write beyond the assignment of language to a medium of personal expression. I have been cognizant that writing does not translate a reality outside itself but, more precisely, allows the emergence of a new reality" (p. 4). In a previous chapter you raised Moraga's questions, "How do we organize ourselves to survive this war? To keep our families, our bodies, our spirits intact?" (Moraga & Anzuldula, 1981, npn) In response to both Simon and Moraga, I say we develop a language of critique, but one in our own voice filled with anger, emotion, and caring.

ROCHELLE: Often in heated class discussions, White students feel under attack because of the emotional mode of expression that some Black students engage in. As the teacher and facilitator I am left with either the choice of silencing Black students, having them speak in a dry, detached style, or utilizing the "teachable moment" and open a discussion on different styles of communication. Of course the discussion is more than a simple talk on different communication styles; instead, it is a view into the historical and social effects on the construction of culture.

An ethic of caring is developing the capacity for empathy. We share with others when we empathize with them and they with us. For example, an interesting conversation took place among several students when I asked them to discuss the class so that I could use their words for a paper I was writing at the time. The discussion eventually turned to the topic of *Hate* and the question would we as a society ever get beyond it? Lisa, an extremely emotional and caring person, sincerely attempts to deal with her Whiteness and understand Black culture.

> Lisa: (White female) I want to touch it [the pain of Black people] and make it better. . . I have to watch it and can't do anything about it. . . my White friends don't understand when I talk about the importance of this class and the fact that I have learned so much.

> Tina: (North Indian female) I understand your pain and I feel bad for it but Black people have to go through the pain everyday of being the other and as much as I feel for what you are experiencing you will never understand the daily pain that Black people experience.

Tina empathized with Lisa's frustration but also was not going to allow Lisa to become the White martyr in the struggle to understand (Tatum, 2003). The students grew into this wonderful "in-your-face-with-the-truth" community. The respect and understanding they had for each other was evident when they joked with Lisa about constantly crying and said they were going to make her a stronger person by the end of the semester. In my classroom I attempt to invoke an ethic of caring in my teaching as well as the ways students interact with each other.

The last theme of the class, Empowerment in Everyday Life, had the purpose of not only to show students how Black women are redefining and empowering themselves and their community, but also how each student has the responsibility to take the learning beyond the class into their everyday life. Tell me, Oshun, have you ever given birth?

OSHUN: From my womb I have given birth to a civilization.

ROCHELLE: Yeah, well, I can't lay claim to a civilization but one night for three hours I felt like I gave birth to the consciousness of 40 students.

OSHUN: Sounds painful.

ROCHELLE: It was. My labor pain lasted four months. But seriously, the birth was actually the fruition of a teaching dream. See, every time I developed a new syllabus for *The African American Woman* I thought about and really wanted to make the final assessment a major class project. Actually a variety show with song, dance, and drama but I could never see how to pull it altogether. Not to mention I was a little scared of tying a large portion of the students grade into one assignment. Well, anyway, as I neared my last semester teaching at State I knew I most likely would never get the chance to teach this particular class again.

OSHUN: There are times when life forces us to take action.

ROCHELLE: And my pending graduation gave me the freedom to pull together everything I hoped I had taught my students. The development of an Afriwomanist pedagogy that had consumed me for two years, more or less, coalesced in the final class project. Understand I didn't want my students to leave with disconnected bits of information. The class, or my pedagogy wasn't meant to present factoids of information but paint a realistic picture of the African American woman. Earlier I talked about the connection of thought and action being a central part of Black feminist thought. Well, my question became how can that connection manifest itself in a semester-length class.

OSHUN: Why a class project?

ROCHELLE: I wanted to see the students bring together and make whole all of the knowledge from the entire semester. I attempted to utilize an alternative mode of assessment to really force the students into new ways of thinking. The celebration as I pictured it would allow students to not only express their individual talents but also concentrate on the specific aspect of the class that had been of greatest significance to their growth. I guess there were two central reasons why I decided on the class project. First, I believe in the importance of public pedagogy—taking what we had learned into the public sphere, beyond the confines of our classroom. I tried to instill in my students the commitment to teach what they had learned throughout the semester. Second, a social justice component had to be part of the project in order for it to be real. Again, it's not just about regurgitating the info back to me but making a difference.

Making the project 40% of the grade I asked the students to design a program celebrating Black women. The only parameters I provided was the time, the last evening of the semester, and that it would be open to the campus community. Many times throughout the semester I regretted my decision. Despite my best efforts and pedagogical strategies most students refused to take the project as seriously as I had hoped they would. Their initial lack of commitment left me with two choices—give failing grades or have a serious, open discussion with the class. I love to expose myself in class.

OSHUN: Isn't that against the law?

ROCHELLE: A goddess with a wicked sense of humor—I love it. Maybe the law of a traditional removed pedagogy, but I prefer to create an open safe environment in my class where we share our feelings so I had no choice but to choose the latter and spend an entire class period expressing my disappointment. I wanted the students to know that although I cared about their learning I was not going to accept their lack of respect for me as an African American woman. I accused them of treating me with less respect based purely on my race and gender thereby proving to me that they were not learning anything. Finally, the really fun part was when I threatened the class with a 25-page research paper in place of the project.

OSHUN: Don't try to make light of what happened. I know you were upset with the class and with yourself for not giving them what they needed.

ROCHELLE: You're right I was upset and I blamed myself for the disaster the class project had turned into more than I blamed the students. But I did not hide my hurt and disappointment from the class. Instead I gave the students an honest expression of my feelings and the power to either further disappoint me or make me a happy teacher.

They did the latter. By some miracle they pulled it together and held a program for the community celebrating Black women. Not only did they have poetry, African and modern dance, skits, and monologues, but they also raised $200 for the local women's shelter.

Learning is and should be messy, confusing, painful. Although at times I doubted the effectiveness of my pedagogy, in the final analysis it was right. The students ultimately developed a sense of social commitment, they cared about the subject, and they took responsibility for their failures and made the needed changes. They acted as a community. Importantly, they began to understand the connectedness of social forces on the perceptions of Black women because they could see their actions as a manifestation of those forces. Ultimately, the students had empowered themselves and in turn empowered me as a teacher.

OSHUN: A synergistic relationship exists between what you as a teacher and they as students receive from the other. As long as both you and the students through your interaction provided the force to keep the synergy alive growth occurs. If either retreated from the interaction the synergistic relationship would cease to exist.

ROCHELLE: I infuse Black feminist thought and critical pedagogy to gain a better understanding of myself, my students, and the ways I design my teaching strategies. I utilize the tenets of Black feminist thought as I try to foster in my students not only a love of knowledge, but also a commitment to political activism and dedication to social change. Although I think I am a good teacher, often in the midst of my inner turmoil I ask myself whether I am leading them far enough. Am I really giving my students what they need, or just disconnected bits of knowledge that will not provide the necessary inner strength? Have I taken my students far enough, to the level of healing necessary to go beyond the *other?* This was perhaps the most important question, and I needed to find the answer.

In the final few minutes of sista dialogue the four Black women who were still there answered that question for me.

● ●

CHINA: Miss Rochelle any other questions that, you know, other issues?

VERONICA: We already covered so much.

ROCHELLE: We covered a lot. I guess I do have one last question and then you guys can go home and I can go to sleep. The ultimate purpose of the study is to not only say what your coping strategies are, but then to say what that has to do with teaching and what that has to do with my pedagogy and how I teach students. So each one of you, start with Miss Stephanie, what is it that you think has been most beneficial to you from a teacher? What has been least beneficial?

GRACE: From you, or a teacher?

CHINA: Just say you.

ROCHELLE: From me. OK.

STEPHANIE: What was the question?

ROCHELLE: What's been most and what's been least beneficial to you as a student and helping you, whether it's get an A, learn something, come to a Black female consciousness, whatever.

CHINA: I'm gonna have to get emotional. I'm failing in my. . . .

STEPHANIE: Before I took your class I didn't think half of this stuff, I mean I did, but it was just like, you know, all right, I'm gonna try to do what I gotta do with it, you know, whatever. And then, it's like after I took the class it was just, all right, I need to think about half this stuff. Don't put the camera on me. Don't put the camera on me.

CHINA: You're beautiful, but smile.

STEPHANIE: What was I saying? Yeah, I just started thinking about little things, I'm not gonna say little things just important things that I should have been thinking about that nobody taught me how to think about it.

ROCHELLE: OK. Miss China.

CHINA: OK, I'm tired and I'm emotional right now, I might start crying.

ROCHELLE: OK, good. People always cry over at my house.

GRACE: Yes.

STEPHANIE: It's not the house but the class.

CHINA: I just feel as though, how am I gonna say it? Basically what I learned, what I'm in the process of learning is, OK put it this way, I feel as though at this very moment in time, it's going to be one of those major milestones in my life that even when I'm 90 in a rocking chair I can always look back. I feel like officially, right now, I'm having a college experience, like I feel like a, I almost have that feeling of being a college student and learning and having that activist feeling of, I'm feeling into myself. I'm coming into myself in a way that I never knew I could come into and that's a direct reflection of you because I never had this feeling in any other class 'cause this is the first time I've ever been in an African American/Women's Studies class and African American Studies really in general and what I haven't learned yet is what you just don't have the answer to, but that nobody has. I haven't learned necessarily why, not why, but how come, like I talked about earlier, I feel picked on. Like you can't make the bullies go away. You can't help, there's a certain part that you just can't do because you're human and you only have the insight of what other people had insight on and what your fellow, and the books you've read and the dissertation you've written, things and all this scholarly stuff, but you can't help, you know there's a certain part that's painful because nobody has the answer. I don't know when I'll stop being picked on, if I'll ever stop being picked on. And I don't even quite understand really why I'm still being picked on and, I know it's because I'm Black and because there's been so many issues and slavery and all this stuff, but I still don't quite understand why. You know, I didn't do anything.

GRACE: China said it very nicely. I think when I took it started with your *Racism and Sexism* class and I think that, in the same vision as China, you gave voice to my Blackness and my womanness together. They didn't know, they knew each other existed, but they were on opposite sides. Say or say one was in my head and one was in my feet and then they like came together halfway and then made it through my mouth like it totally like you just gave voice to something that I think that I was so at conflict with. Inner-like conflict and I just first, thank you. But along with what China was saying, I don't think that anything in your class could have been done, could have been done differently or you taught me something different. Just the things that I guess I'm still searching for, I'm still struggling with. Those are just things of everyday life. I don't know. Even today, even in this class, I still like, it's like every time I take your class, it's just more open space that I can go and explore. We can't do every day or like in, 'cause everybody wants you to forget. Everybody's trying to. . .

ROCHELLE: Push it away.

GRACE: Yeah, exactly. Not acknowledge it at all and I can do that in your class. So I don't think there's anything that I would want to do differently. Another thing I really like is how you show us through women's, Black women's perspectives, or women period. You show us the different people's perspectives and their own written words and you don't just teach us how this person is this way, this person is that way, this person said this, this person said this, but you give us women's heartfelt pieces of work. Do you know what I mean, their words so we can connect with that and take and feel our own thing.

VERONICA: You're not gonna put that camera on me. . .Wow. The ladies articulated so well. A lot of things that I feel also that, as she said, the giving voice to the black and the female and making them come together as one. I find myself more now, since the class, forcing that issue whenever it slides to the Black male or it slides to the White woman, I want it to stay on the issues facing Black females. I now realize that my issues are different from that of a White woman and my issues are somewhat different of that of a Black male so, of course, I thank you for that. Wow. I can't even think of anything else. Just fried my brain.

I mean, there's just finding out that there are other people who deal with, I think that was the most important thing for me today and through the class. Like she said, the fact that we have a forum finally to voice, and people care to hear what it was that we were feeling as opposed to me arguing about it in some COM course. It's just a Black chick screaming about something again. In this class, in this course, I felt as though what I had to say mattered and when I would walk out of that classroom, I felt like I had made a point in it. It somehow got across to somebody and that was important to me. There's not many opportunities you get at State to connect with people and so, through this class and through this, I actually met some people. I don't know, things I wished to change, I guess the only thing that, which is really nothing to change about the course, but like they said, just I guess putting some answers to a lot of those questions that I still have. A lot of those identity questions, moving further into Black consciousness. Trying to understand the other side, trying to be open minded, trying to be fair when it seems almost impossible. For those things that I feel like I've been given. . .to deal with myself. I now know I have a foundation from which to start to build my own Black consciousness, my own female consciousness and bring them together to where they impact me so that I can then turn around and impact people. The most important thing I got out of this class was that it's so important for me to go back and get them little Black girls.

ALL: Yes.

VERONICA: It's so important because a lot of us didn't have that and a lot of the Black girls right now don't have it. It's important for me to get them, you know, while they're young as opposed to, so they don't go through this. They'll have some more different issues, but at least those will have some balance for them instead of just finding out now. So that's it.

ROCHELLE: Very good. This is called a slow pan. And it's over.

Transition
Reflecting on Self

> Many subjects touched my soul, many inspired thought, anger, concern for the future and growth. Looking back, the discussions and readings about language, oppression, interracial dating, the American Indian, the Chicana woman and the "place" of the African American woman influenced my being the most. My mood of the day was determined by how well our discussion went in class. If the discussion was frustrating, I was frustrated all day long. If I was enlightened by the class discussion, all day I felt a glow of newly discovered knowledge. (log entry from Racism and Sexism 103)

Patricia Hill Collins (1991) argues that a Black "way of knowing" is one that relates learned knowledge to actual experience; either personal experience or that of the community in general. I often chastise my students when I feel that they are not moving back and forth between personal and learned knowledge, but simply stuck in their personal experiences (hooks, 1994). I do this until I remember that I most often relate to and engage with learned knowledge first from a personal standpoint.

When I teach *Racism and Sexism* 103, and *The African American Woman* 102, I do so from a Black feminist perspective. My mantra in both classes is "the interlocking systems of class, race, and gender" and as a class we look at what Gloria Wade-Gayles calls the *Triple Jeopardy* of Black women (Wade-Gayles, 1984). I "force" the students to take their knowledge to the next level through a critically analysis of assigned and suggested readings. As a class we spend time looking at the social constructions of the other, oppression, domination, the politics of epistemology, dichotomies between Black women and White women, ideology, media representations, etc. We struggle (as learners and teacher) through Patricia Hill Collins's "Toward an Afrocentric Feminist Epistemology" and "Toward a Socialist Theory of Racism" by Cornel West.

hooks argues that many of the Black female students in her class do not know the language of feminism and have never had a Women's Studies course (hooks, 1994). I also see the struggle of my Black female students and their attempt to engage in the material from a theoretical perspective. The White female students have taken other Women's Studies courses and are typically more familiar with the jargon. For African American students the class *The African American Woman* is usually their first Women's Studies class and one that especially teaches from a Black Women's perspective. It is always interesting to see them struggle with the concepts and find ways to relate to the material from an analytical standpoint. When I question the Black women why they have never had a Women's Studies course I usually get the same answer—"My issues are not discussed."

I am often amazed at the conservative thinking of young students. When they enter the class they have a bag of preconceived, false notions that they fight to hold onto. I always feel it is my job as a critical teacher to at the very least shake up the bag and hopefully empty it by semester's end.

How do you teach a class from a feminist perspective? hooks (1994) states that "feminist scholarship must change ways of seeing, talking, and thinking if we are to speak to the various audiences, the different subjects who may be present in one location" (p. 112). The diverse ethnicities represented and ideological views in my class often lead to heated discussions and it is during that time when as a teacher I feel that the most learning is taking place. "Confronting one another across differences means that we must change ideas about how we learn; rather than fearing conflict we have to find ways to use it as a catalyst for new thinking, for growth" (hooks, 1994, p. 131). I have found out that the differences are not always in the classroom, but most often are internal struggles of the students who are usually not even aware or able to name their internal conflict. Once aware of the struggle, once they can name it, they experience the beginning of the type of freedom education should provide.

> I am enlightened. I have been in a war with myself for so many years not even knowing the sides, not knowing the beginning from the end. Nonetheless, the end has came and the truce is made. . . . In the same manner in which I celebrate my culture, my astounding darkness, I will celebrate my womanhood. I take with me this celebration of self-knowledge and self-assurance. I internalize the beauty of my completeness. I recognize this complete nature and its only now that I can go on to help others and to see others life conditions as my own. I am complete. I am a Black woman. (log entry from *Racism and Sexism* 103)

seven

The End of My Beginning

OSHUN: Rochelle, after all is said and done, researched and analyzed, debated and discussed, theorized and practiced, has your pain gone away? In other words, did you theorize away the pain?

ROCHELLE: No. There is a part of me that feels that I have written pages of rubbish. The only thing I have theorized is my way into a book and perhaps tenure. Beyond that I don't know.

OSHUN: Aren't you being a little too hard on yourself? Putting yourself up to some infeasible standard of perfection?

ROCHELLE: Maybe, but I feel deep within my soul that the standard has to be reached. It's not just a matter of finishing this book. You know, fodder for the cannon. What I've been attempting to talk about for the last 118 pages is survival and strength. Making it despite all odds.

OSHUN: Well haven't you been? You did not provide a recipe for survival but who can? I believe a cookbook of survival is futile. What you used last week as a weapon against attack may not work today.

ROCHELLE: You're right but still. . .

OSHUN: I know you wanted to provide a prescription for racism to your readers.

ROCHELLE: When I first thought of this topic, a lifetime ago, that is exactly what I had envisioned. I wanted Black women especially to be able to read this and find the pages filled with what they needed to survive. Answer their questions. But I guess I was making myself this omnipotent person.

OSHUN: Exactly! So step back from that original desire and tell me what you have actually accomplished.

ROCHELLE: I showed how one person can research and write about Black women and education. This book is from my perspective filled with all of its biases. The women I interviewed are individuals and what they say and how they feel about being Black is their perspective. Their words are not meant to be generalized to an entire group.

OSHUN: Tell me what you have learned from writing *Sista Talk*.

ROCHELLE: So much. I now understand that the writing of a book is a process and a time of growth. If I were to start over with what I know now the first three chapters would be different. Even the questions I have now are not the ones I had in the beginning. When I started to reread to make the final revisions I found myself changing and deleting so much that I had to stop.

OSHUN: Education as a verb.

ROCHELLE: I cannot pinpoint a beginning or an end to the conceptualization of my subject. Even before I provided my editor with a book proposal, the topic had been incubating inside of me. Actually the subject is grounded in knowledge of self so as I change and grow and learn so does the outcome of this topic which is why I had a difficult time with the concept of a concluding chapter.

OSHUN: In place of conclusion why don't we just call it the "for now" thoughts on what you did.

ROCHELLE: Yes. To answer the question "Did I theorize away the pain," I can say yes, for now. Through knowledge and life experiences, the pain is not gone but I understand it and can better deal with it. At the same time I know that living in this world as a Black woman brings constant pain of spirit and soul. I also know that living as a Black woman who is cognizant of a womanist way of being also brings the strength I need. I am aware of the influence my race, class, and gender has on my pedagogy.

I have learned from this experience, but not everything I wanted to, and I have not taught everything I wanted to teach in this book. I do not think I have come close because there is so much out there to know and to change. Yet, I know, that despite all the things I (at times) allow to push me down, as a Black Woman I found the courage to speak and write my truth.

Finally I have learned that although my journey is just beginning I am prepared.

OSHUN: Do you still need me?

ROCHELLE: Oshun I will always need you. When we begin this conversation I was lost, unsure of where to go and how to proceed. Despite my dedication to helping my students find their internal power I had lost mine with no idea of how to get it back. It's funny but even as I was writing this I was still struggling with the same doubts and incompleteness that I wrote about for Jake and Michael. I thank you for helping me to touch that ancient and knowing part of my spirit.

OSHUN: Remember me, the African goddess of voluptuous beauty, the goddess of love and beauty, the goddess of fertility, the female master of strategy. I am the sweet and sour taste of life. I will always be a part of you.

Oshun, created with music and brought to life with rhythm and soul, a goddess with the strength to move the paradigm beyond the margins. Oshun and Rochelle wrote their truth. One gave voice to the silent. The other gave life to forgotten memories. Together they are whole.

Appendix A
The Methodology of Sista Dialogue: Safe Spaces for Being Us

OSHUN: Creating a safe space to work through issues that are emotional is paramount to any study and especially one that delves into concepts of self and survival. So, did you allow the women to bask in safety for at least a brief time?

ROCHELLE: That was my goal and I do believe I succeeded in doing just that. The central method I used was based on the group conversation method which is a culturally relevant qualitative ethnographic strategy used by King and Mitchell in *Black Mother to Sons* (1995). They state that the group conversation method developed by DuBois and Li (1971) to "reduce social tensions" was revised and adapted by them to "help participants identify shared experiences and to facilitate the discussion of highly personal or deeply felt emotional issues" (King, 1995, p. 3). The group conversation method is a way of knowing and understanding the reality of Black life. In this method African American literature is used to initiate a group discussion and critical reflection about participants' shared experiences.

OSHUN: How did you choose the women of sista dialogue?

ROCHELLE: The participants were chosen based on their proven ability to grapple with issues pertinent to Black women and those discussed in my study. In fact, the reason I decided to use past students was because they were better able to enter the discussion on a more substantive level then those Black women not acquainted with Black feminist consciousness. In addition, the women selected for this study were those I knew to be both introspective and able to relate personal issues to larger, ideological issues. Since my classes delve into the constructions of race and identity, the women were familiar with Black feminism, dichotomous thought, stereotypes, Black female devaluation, and so on.

OSHUN: You already had a relationship with these women. Wasn't that setting up a conflict?

ROCHELLE: My position in the group was that of participant and researcher. A central part of this method is that the researcher is not removed from the study. According to King (1995), this method "elicits reciprocal dialogue and creates the conditions for the researcher to learn with the participants about what 'we' do and to reflect on why 'we' do it in a manner that is akin to Douglas's (1985) creative interviewing strategy in which the interviewer engages participants in a mutual search for self-understanding" (p. 5). As previously mentioned the capacity for empathy is paramount to the group participants opening up to the researcher. If I acted as strictly researcher the richness of group discussion would not be realized. On the other hand, complete participation would have served to silence the students and turn sista dialogue into just another classroom discussion with me as teacher. Therefore I worked to maintain a balance throughout the discussion.

OSHUN: Balance or control?

ROCHELLE: A balance that I grounded in awareness. In the creation of this balance two things were considered. The first consideration was my role in the dialogue. Based on the fact that I am considerably older than my participants (18 to 23 years olds) and possess a different degree of theoretical understanding and life experiences, I negotiated with the participants and with myself regarding my "place" in the group. My purpose was not to silence or teach, but to engage with the students in their learning and achieving of a "higher" level of inquiry. Prior to the start of the group I explained to the participants the topic of my research and the general direction I wanted the sista dialogue to proceed. The women individually directed the conversation discussing subjects that were important to them. Occasionally when we veered and remained off subject for what I thought was too long I played teacher and directed the conversation back to the topic. More often then not the women policed each other for the sake of my research.

Since the students selected had been in my classes before (some students may have taken two or three), I needed to ensure that their voice came through in the discussion and not what they had heard me say in the past. This second consideration proved to be a nonissue because the women selected to be in the study are those that I knew to be strong willed and on their way to realizing an individual standpoint. As their teacher and mentor I had witnessed the intellectual growth of each one of these woman. I also had provided them with, in my pedagogy, the knowledge of and commitment to those issues and concerns relevant to Black women.

Sista dialogue as a methodology grew out of the four characteristics of a Black feminist epistemology as delineated by Patricia Hill Collins (1991) that I discussed in greater detail earlier. First, the participants of the sista dialogue are young Black women in the midst of an attempt to come into their womanhood and Black feminist consciousness. These women brought to the discussion concrete experience as a criterion of meaning as expressed by Collins as the first characteristic of a Black feminist epistemology. The purpose of my study did not allow men or women of any other race to participate because Black women are the only ones that can define their own standpoint.

The essence of sista dialogue is the "use of dialogue in assessing knowledge claims" (Collins, 1991, p. 212), the second characteristic of a Black Feminist epistemology. For six hours, a group of women discussed, debated, questioned, and analyzed our way into a deeper level of understanding ourselves and Black women. Talking to each woman individually would not have afforded the opportunity for the women to build upon each others' experiences, nor would it allow for us to "help" each other articulate the tacit knowledge each already possessed. I was not concerned that sista dialogue would become a "group think" because I knew the women involved were equally as strong in their convictions but also mature enough to listen to and learn from opinions that might be different.

The third characteristic of a Black feminist epistemology, the ethic of caring, is illuminated in the women chosen to participate. These women, although from a variety of socioeconomic backgrounds, have in common their commitment to a spiritual growth as young Black women. They care about and question what happens to them personally and what befalls all Black women. Notwithstanding that the women are at different levels of self-knowledge and do not all define themselves as a Black feminist, they are reaching to achieve a social and personal consciousness in their Black femaleness.

The three components of an ethic of caring—individual uniqueness, appropriateness of emotions in dialogue, and capacity for empathy—discussed in the previous section are a necessary part of a research design in an African American epistemology. A research design must take into account that African Americans are not monolithic in thought or action. The research design must also consider emotions as a factor in both the data collection and the data analysis. Finally, the research design in an African American epistemological framework must be aware that in order to establish a relationship with the study participants the researcher must develop the capacity for empathy.

The fourth characteristic of a Black feminist epistemology, personal accountability gave me the freedom to not fear the women in sista dialogue would fall into group think.

OSHUN: Meaning.

ROCHELLE: The women took it upon themselves to make sure that they expressed their individuality when needed and to speak as a group when needed. They knew each other well enough and felt comfortable enough with the subject and with me that a level of accountability to "get it all out" was a major part of our dialogue.

OSHUN: Ultimately what is it you wanted to do with sista dialogue?

ROCHELLE: I wanted to tell my story and the stories of my Black female students as we search for meaning and develop strategies to remain complete.

My search is part of a three-year self-study, culminating in a focus group, into how I became the teacher I am today. But when I relate this to others they give me that look, you know the look I mean—one that insinuates the lack of a "true" intellectual endeavor, something that has no meaning outside of the story itself. With shaded eye—so I cannot see into their thoughts—they utter, "Oh, how *interesting*," or worse yet, "Uhmmm, I see."

OSHUN: You must remember that writing this book is a game and like any game there are rules. In many ways you are breaking the rules by researching yourself (an *n* of one is unacceptable) and writing in dialogue with me, your alter ego. I am able to help those who choose to listen, circumvent the accepted staid format, but only when they know the rules of the game are they able to use those very rules against their critics.

ROCHELLE: But will I give them power over my voice if I do it that way?

OSHUN: So much of the internal struggle you are experiencing comes from this need you have to say things the way you feel and yet to be intellectually accepted by your peers as a *true academician*. You are letting them control your actions. Don't. Instead, speak with their words only long enough to make your point known in a way that those who hold the "power" can understand and accept. Your study is personal, therefore it is heuristic. You and your participants are intimately connected with the subject under study. Heuristic inquiry asks, "What is my experience of this phenomenon and the essential of others who also experience this phenomenon intensely?" (Patton, 1990, p. 71). In heuristic research, the researcher and the coresearchers must have personal experience and an intense interest in the phenomena under study. Because of this, the relationship is more than researcher and researched; instead, a connectedness develops between researcher and participants in their shared efforts to interpret the essence of a critical human experience. As opposed to object and subject a synergistic relationship develops bringing about coresearchers. Douglas and Moustakas (1984) posit that in heuristic inquiry discovery comes from "a kind of being wide open in surrender to the thing itself, a recognition that one must relinquish control and be tumbled about with the newness and drama of a searching focus that is taking over life" (as cited in Patton, 1990, p. 72).

Heuristic inquiry legitimizes and places at the forefront personal experiences, reflections, and insights of you, the researcher. Through heuristic inquiry you began a journey of understanding the phenomena as you travel with and into an experience with coresearchers. Patton (1990) posits that "The rigor of heuristic inquiry comes from systematic observation of and dialogue with self and others, as well as in-depth interviewing" (p. 72) of others and has the potential for disclosing truth. Through self-search and dialogue, one cultivates a comprehensive knowledge.

ROCHELLE: In this study I blend the related areas of phenomenology and heuristic inquiry. While many researchers utilizing phenomenology focus on analyzing an experience from the perspective of the researched, heuristics simultaneously emphasizes the connectedness between researcher and what is being researched, leading to "depictions of essential meanings and portrayals of the intrigue and personal significance that involve the search to know" (Patton, 1990, p. 73). While phenomenology may unwittingly objectify the person in the process of descriptive analysis, heuristic research participants maintain their voice through collaboration between the researcher and the coresearcher (Douglas & Moustakas, 1985; Patton, 1990). Heuristic research epitomizes the phenomenological emphasis on meaning and knowing through personal experience, exemplifying the way in which the researched is not objectified in qualitative inquiry.

OSHUN: You can speak with their words!

ROCHELLE: Yes, but like the mere mortals in the story of the Celestial City, I often feel that even when I use the language of those who attempt to colonize my mind my subject and I are still not deemed important. I struggle to find that space where I can place in a theoretical context what and why I do what I do and remain true to my own voice.

OSHUN: You talk about others needing to break out of their established paradigms, but yet you place yourself in one and seemingly refuse to or can't shatter the illusion of a *one right way* to do this. Richardson (1998) states that

> The core of postmodernism is the *doubt* that any method or theory, discourse or genre, tradition or novelty, has a universal and general claim as the "right" or privileged form of authoritative knowledge. Postmodernism *suspects* all truth claims of masking and serving particular interests in local, cultural, and political struggles. But postmodernism does not automatically reject conventional methods of knowing and telling as false or archaic. Rather, it opens those standard methods to inquiry and introduces new methods, which are also, then, subject to critique. (p. 348)

Accordingly, you are situated in your writing and need to speak from that place, not as an objective, "disembodied omniscient narrator[s] claiming universal, atemporal general knowledge" about your subject but instead you must question and critique the "metanarrative of scientific objectivity. . . as situated speaker. . . engaged in knowing/telling about the world as [you] perceive it" (Richardson, 1998, p. 348).

ROCHELLE: Am I not now being a "disembodied omniscient narrator" by choosing to write in a fictitious conversation with a goddess? Am I placing myself outside of myself in order to talk about what is inside?

OSHUN: Or are you simply using a rhetorical strategy which is both engaging and challenging. . .

ROCHELLE: . . . as I write about, and others read the words of, my journey and the journey of my Black female students? Sister Audre Lorde (1996c) said:

> I have come to understand over and over again that what is most important to me must be spoken, made verbal and shared, even at the risk of having it bruised or misunderstood. (p. 40)

I walk a fine line between the knower and the teller in the way in which I go about relating this story. Will I be misunderstood? Probably. Will my words be deemed as unimportant? Definitely, by some people. Regardless, I provide a "*narrative of self*" through "*evocative representations*" which "employs literary devices to re-create lived experience and evoke emotional responses" through which we "experience the self-reflexive and transformational process of self-creation" (Richardson, 1998, p 355). Evocative representation allows me to "feel it," "play with it," "re-create it," and "touch it." "It" being the personal story of living as a Black woman.

Is my personal experience fodder for theory and inquiry? Or is it just the lamenting of another "angry Black woman?" I stand the risk of having the data that I collect from others, as well as that which is purely personal, viewed as irrelevant. According to Clandinin and Connelly (1998), the criticism against personal experience in inquiry is really about the "politics of epistemology" and what is defined as "acceptable knowledge and inquiry" (p. 153).

OSHUN: And what is acceptable epistemology?

ROCHELLE: According to Clandinin and Connelly (1998), there are two contentions with the personal experience method. The first is sociological and grounded in the belief that "social organizations and structures rather than people and experience are the appropriate starting points for social science inquiry" (p. 153). This means that social structures construct people and not that people construct social structures, which takes away agency making humans nothing but mere cogs in somebody else's machinery. On the other hand, another argument is that experience is too "comprehensive, too holistic, and, therefore, an insufficiently analytical term to permit useful inquiry" (Clandinin & Connelly, 1998, p. 153).

Both arguments are, of course, grounded in a modernist paradigm, which seeks only one story, one truth, and importantly, one voice. In contrast, my research has many stories, truths, and voices, each meaningful for the narrative of a Black woman's journey.

OSHUN: Speak about the social world.

ROCHELLE: Okay. The personal experience method provides an avenue into the social world I write and theorize about. It would be impossible to write about Black women in general, and my research participants in particular, without telling my own story as a Black woman and how that story has constructed me. The connections between my two selves—teacher and Black female—are inseparable. To try to do so is to create a false binary. Clandinin and Connelly (1998) state:

> One of the special powers of personal experience methods is that their connection goes beyond theories, researchers, and practitioners, to the life community within which these traditional parties to inquiry relate. Personal experience research is a form of public inquiry that has the potential for transcending the specialties of research in particular subject fields. It does this because personal experience methods connect with fundamental human experience. Personal experience methods are human methods. (p. 174)

I turn in all directions when personal experience is used. First, I look within to find that which makes me who I am—those things that are so much a part of me that they are seldom, if ever, articulated such as feelings, beliefs, morals, hopes, dreams, fears, and prejudices. Second, I look outward to understand the environment, define the "reality" of myself and those I speak with. Understanding the placement of individuals within the "web of reality" forces me to examine those social structures which work to define the being of the person.

Finally, as I analyze my personal experience and those of my coresearchers, I place everything in context by looking backward and forward. It's not just taking a slice of my life without regard to my past or future. Instead, I try to figure out what has happened in my past to bring me to my current place and how that relates to where I hope to go in the future. Simply put, it's a holistic point of departure into the present experiences of me but one still able to be analyzed.

My concern for the education of Black people is paramount to who I am. At the same time, there is an internal dialogue I am having with how to best design a transformative pedagogy I know is needed.

OSHUN: What turned you on about *evocative representation* and where do you think it can lead your study?

ROCHELLE: Come on, the title itself means it has got to be great! But what I really liked was that through evocative representations I can have fun with this. I can send copies to my little sister, who is extremely smart but not steeped in academic lingo and she can read it, enjoy it while she is reading, and learn from it. This form of theorizing and analyzing allows me to break out of the assigned box and utilize the methods I feel are more useful in getting my point across. There are various forms in evocative representation and the one I choose was mixed genre, which allowed me to utilize and develop that which is best suited for my purpose. I have allowed myself, through mixed genre, to use poetry, prose, academic jargon, and a conversation with you to tell my story.

OSHUN: Not only can you say use literature and art, but how you use them is the key. Richardson (1998) called mixed genre a "postmodernist deconstruction of triangulation" because it does not triangulate; it crystallizes. Close your eyes and envision a crystal. Feel the smooth multifaceted surface between the sharp edges. Now hold it up to the sun so you can see the brilliance in its many colors. Can you feel the power and magic that emanates from the crystal? Do you feel its warmth? Its vibrancy? That is what the use of mixed genre brings to your writing. Remember the 'one right way' you were having a hissy fit about earlier? There is no one correct way to cut a crystal. Instead, each variation in the cut brings new depth and distinct gradients of color. And so are there many ways to tell your story, each one bringing new depth and distinct gradients of color.

ROCHELLE: I'm feeling you and I'm lovin' the freedom.

Appendix B
The Boring but Necessary Stuff

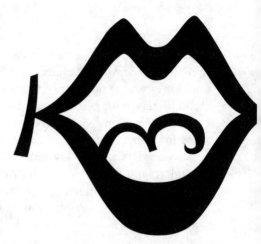

The Participants*

I did not have to search through my memory more than a few moments to decide who I wanted to participate in sista dialogue. I chose eight past Black female students from my class *The African American Woman* and *Racism and Sexism* who exhibited the qualities I wanted to discuss in this study. All of the women, despite their struggles, are succeeding academically in college and place an emphasis on academic excellence. They had been active participants in class, engaging in class discussion and creating a challenging learning environment for all students.

1. Grace. I have known Grace since the summer of 1997 when she took *Racism and Sexism* 103 from me. After that class I kept in touch with Grace and interviewed her for a paper presented at the American Educational Research Association 1998 annual meeting in San Diego, California. Grace took *The African American Woman* this semester and also worked as my teaching assistant.** Throughout the two years we met occasionally on campus for lunch and Grace attended several of the parties I gave students at my home. She also participated in the preliminary focus group I held at the insistence of several students who were unable to participate in the final study. Grace's parents are divorced and during conversations of the last two years she constantly mentions her mother but seldom remarks on her father. A graduating senior, Grace is from a small rural town and has one older brother who suffers from a debilitative brain disease, which has led Grace to question her own existence and good health. Grace identifies herself as Black from a working-class family.

2. Carole. I first had Carole in *The African American Woman* class during spring 1998. Carole then acted as my teaching assistant for *The African American Woman* during fall 1998 and spring 1999. Carole is majoring in education and plans to be an elementary school teacher. For her age, 19, I have

---

*All names of the participants have been changed to protect privacy.
** My teaching assistants do not get credit or monetary compensation.

found Carole to be extremely mature and able to question and think at levels of abstraction some "adults" never reach. Carole grew up in the suburbs of a major city the youngest of four children. She defines herself as middle-class and biracial with her mother from Switzerland and father from Liberia.

3. Stephanie. Stephanie was a student in *The African American Woman* the first time I taught it at State in the Spring of 1997. She also took *Racism and Sexism* during the summer of 1998. Stephanie is the youngest, 21, of eight children and identifies herself as a Black American. She is a graduating senior and although intelligent she is extremely shy and unsure of herself. I noticed in class that although Stephanie did not talk much she was a committed and dedicated learner and always willing to stretch the boundaries of her knowledge.

4. Veronica. Veronica was a student in *The African American Woman* in spring 1998, the first semester after she had transferred to State from a school in the northeast. Veronica always was active in class and discussions and never afraid to push herself or other to new levels of understandings. She identifies herself as African American from a working-class background and is the second oldest, 20, of four siblings. Veronica is from an urban area of a major city with divorced parents.

5. China. China was a student in *The African American Woman* in spring 1999 and identifies herself as African American. She is an only child and her parents are divorced. Like the other women from divorced parents, China is extremely close to her mother and mentions her father only in passing. China describes her home environment as extremely urban and herself as loving to be the center of attention. She was often the excitement in class, challenging herself and other students to tackle issues of racism and sexism. Although I had known China the least amount of time and therefore had the least amount of interaction with her I included her in sista dialogue because she was bright and inquisitive, and had just began to think about issues related to Black women since taking my class.

6. Jennifer. Jennifer is the middle of three siblings and describes herself as African American from an upper middle-class family. She is a master's student in the College of Education and a student teacher intern in the Professional Development School, which I am a part of. I have known Jennifer since fall of 1998 in the capacity of mentor/mentee, watching her struggle with understanding herself as a teacher and a Black woman and the relationship between the two.

7. Natasha. Natasha, a graduating senior, is from a single female-headed household and describes her home environment as urban. Natasha was in *The African American Woman* during spring 1998, displaying an analytical mind and questioning attitude. She also was the positive one of the group, talking about the need to maintain a positive attitude for the sake of mental health.

8. Stacy. Stacy is a junior and from an urban middle-class background. She identifies herself as Black Haitian and is involved in both parts of her ethnicity. Stacy was my student in *The African American Woman* during spring 1998.

I gave the participants a Biographical Sketch questionnaire asking for basic information, wanting to find out how the students identified themselves. For example, on ethnicity did they put Black, African American, or in the case of Carole biracial. Also, the socioeconomic standing of their family was a self-report. I did not have economic parameters to help them figure this question out. Interestingly, when Carole was filling out this section she asked what was the difference between working-class, middle-class, and upper middle-class to which China answered, "Middle-class is when your family goes on vacation to Disney World."

The Location

The State University is a large university located in a predominantly White working-class to middle-class rural community. The closest major city is a three-hour drive so the school feels very isolated. The minority population on campus and in the city is less than five percent. The campus environment is not welcoming to minority students, practicing a form of benign neglect and at other times racist acts of silencing and aggression. There are no Black nightclubs, Black radio stations, or Black restaurants in the area. Ethnic hair care products are next to impossible to find with most Black students sending away to home when a product is needed. Although there is a Black undergraduate organization, most students do not get actively involved. This is probably due to the lack of organization the group has experienced during the last three years.

The women of sista dialogue were chosen because each is attempting to understand their Black female self. They are self-reflective, intelligent women who attempted to theorize away the pain of being Black women.

The Research Methods

Even though the majority of this book endeavors to analyze the various components of Black women's lives, its essence or driving force is my inner exploration into the essential factors in good teaching of Black women about Black women. Toward this end I have used action research, the "study of a social situation with a view to improving the quality of action within it," as one of the methodologies (Altrichter, Posch, & Somekh, 1993, p. 4). Cochran-Smith and Lytle (1993) define action research as the "systematic, intentional inquiry by teachers about their own school and classroom work" (p. 23). These authors go on to state that teacher action research informs and is informed by all teacher research past and present. I tried to make sense of what I was doing in the classroom that led me to help my Black female students reach a level of consciousness I only dreamed of at their age. Hahn (1991) points out that "[t]he teacher's knowledge is conceived in the classroom and it lives in the classroom (as cited in Cochran-Smith & Lytle, 1993, p. 39).

One of the essential motives for doing action research lies in the desire to transform teaching and learning. According to Altrichter et al. (1993), there are four important objectives or criteria for judging the quality of action research: to develop and improve practice through research in the interest of all those concerned; to develop the knowledge and practical understanding of those involved in the research process; to develop the professional knowledge of teachers as a whole; and to develop and improve education as a discipline (p. 207).

Although Altrichter et al. and Cochran-Smith and Lytle provide a good jumping-off point in understanding and doing action research, I am not feeling the critical or radical component necessary for student–teacher transformation. On the other hand, *critical* action research is "grounded on an emancipatory system of meaning" and "is essential to the realization of [a] democratic. . . workplace" and "bringing the research process to critical consciousness" (Kincheloe, 1991, p. 104). Critical action research uses the teacher's awareness of subjugated knowledge and marginalized groups to engage in research, which critiques, questions, debates, and revolutionizes the established ways of schooling, learning, and teaching. Critical action research does not silence the voice of the student, as they perceive their own reality, but instead heuristically acknowledges its importance.

Although sista dialogue revealed some very painful issues for all of the women involved, I found that trust (for me as a researcher) never became an issue. The participants of course signed the required Informed Consent document but interestingly several wanted their real names used in the final analysis. For ethical reasons, it was paramount to the success of my study that I collaborate in a negotiated evaluation of the situation with the participants. Thus, it was very important that all activities use ethical criteria in their development. Action research is based on the belief that effective change in practice is only possible in a cooperation with all the participants in the situation—it cannot be achieved against their will, which of course holds for all types of research as well. Therefore, research methods should help to develop democratic and cooperative relationships. The participants of the focus group were involved in helping me develop the parameters of sista dialogue. Each offered suggestions and criticism throughout the process.

Action research addresses this problem in two ways. First, research methods are governed by ethical principles, in particular negotiation, confidentiality, and participants' control. I said earlier that research techniques may be used only with the consent of all those concerned. In classroom research, the

pupils are told the aims of the investigation and are asked for their cooperation. If the methods of data collection are not acceptable, alternative proce-
dures have to be negotiated. In my research, the classroom as a negotiated
space between teacher and student was an important variable; one considered
throughout the investigation. Altrichter et al. (1993) state that before an interview, the pupils are told what use will be made of the data, and afterward
they are given the opportunity to think over what they have said and asked
if the data can be used in the research. Member checking, an integral part of
qualitative research, is an important part of the ultimate validation of research
data gathered (Cochran-Smith & Lytle, 1993; Patton 1990).

The confidentiality rule in action research states that the data are the
property of those from whom they originate and therefore have to be treated
confidentially and may not be passed on to others without permission. The
collaborative effort between the researcher and those being researched extends beyond the actual point of data collection to the analysis and writings
of the research findings. All participants agree to findings, or at the very least
each provide their individual interpretations of said data.

Ensuring the negotiation and confidentiality of the research project participants' control is the third component of ethical principles that govern action research. Altrichter et al. assert that those who participate in the situation
keep control of the research. This ethical principle is of great importance in
building trust between researcher and coresearchers. It is necessary that control of a research project remains in the hands of those who have to live with
its consequences. This principle requires the researcher to guide the action
but not dominate it.

References

Akbar, N. (1984). *Chains and images of psychological slavery*. Jersey City, NJ: New Mind Productions.

Albertson, E. (1996). *The complete i ching for the millions*. Los Angeles: Sherbourne Press.

Altrichter, H., Posch, P., & Somekh, B. (1993). *Teachers investigate their work: An introduction to the methods of action research*. New York: Routledge.

Ani, M. (1994). *Yurugu: An African-centered critique of European cultural thought and behavior*. Trenton, NJ: Africa Free World Press.

Argyis, C., Putman, R., & McLain Smith, D. (1985). *Action science: Concepts, methods, and skills for research intervention*. San Francisco: Jossey-Bass.

Asante, M. K. (1991). The Afrocentric idea in education. *Journal of Negro Education*, 60, 170–179.

Asante, M. K., & D. Atwater. (1986). The rhetorical condition as symbolic structure in discourse. *Communication Quarterly*, 34, 170–177.

Beale, F. (1995). Double jeopardy: To be Black and female. In B. Guy-Sheftall (Ed.), *Words of fire: An anthology of African American feminist thought* (pp. 146–155). New York: The New York Press. (Original work published in 1970)

Bennett, L., Jr. (1993). *Before the Mayflower: A history of Black America* (6th ed.). New York: Penguin Books.

Boateng, F. (1991). Combating deculturalization of the African-American child in the public school system: A multicultural approach. In K. Lomotey (Ed.), *Going to school: The African-American experience* (pp.73–84). Albany: State University of New York Press.

Bowles, S., & Gintis, H. (1976). *Schooling in capitalist America: Educational reform and the contradictions of economic life*. New York: Basic Books.

Boyd, J. A. (1998). *Can I get a witness: For sisters, when the blues is more than a song*. New York: Dutton.

Boykin, A.W. (2000). The challenges of cultural socialization in the schooling of African American elementary school children: Exposing the hidden curriculum. In W. Watkins, J. Lewis, & V. Chou (Eds.) *Race and education* (pp. 190–191). Needham, MA: Allyn & Bacon.

Brown, E. B. (1994). Womanist consciousness: Maggie Lena Walker and the independent order of Saint Luke. In V. L. Ruiz. & E. C. Dubios (Eds.), *Unequal sister: A multicultural reader in U. S. women's history* (pp. 268–283). New York: Routledge. (Original published in 1989)

Clandinin, J. D., & Connelly, M. F. (1998). Personal experience methods. In N. K. Denzin & Y. S. Lincoln (Eds.), *Collecting and interpreting qualitative materials* (pp. 150–178). Thousand Oaks, CA: Sage.

Cochran-Smith, M., & Lytle, S. L. (1993). *Inside outside: Teacher research and knowledge.* New York: Teachers College Press.

Collins, P. H. (1991). *Black feminist thought: Knowledge, consciousness and the politics of empowerment.* New York: Routledge.

Cross, W. E. (1991). *Shades of black: Diversity on African-American identity.* Philadelphia: Temple University Press.

Davis, A. (1998). *Blues legacies and Black feminism.* New York: Pantheon Books.

Dill Thorton, B. (1994). Race, class, and gender: Prospects for an all-inclusive sisterhood. In L. Stone (Ed.), *The education feminism reader* (pp. 42–56). New York: Routledge. (Original work published in 1983)

Douglas, B. G. & Moustakas, C. (1985). Heuristic inquiry: The internal search to know. *Human Psychology* 25 (3): 39–55.

Dubois, W. E. B. (1961). *Souls of black folk.* Greenwich, CT: Fawcett Publications. (Original work published in 1903)

duCille, A. (1994). The occult of true black womanhood: Critical demeanor and Black feminist studies. *Signs: Journal of Women in Culture & Society* 19 (3) 591–629.

Ellison, R. (1972). *Invisible man.* New York: Vintage Books.

Ellsworth, E. (1992). Why doesn't this feel empowering? Working through the repressive myths of critical pedagogy. In L. Stone (Ed.), *The education feminism reader* (pp. 300–327). New York: Routledge. (Original work published in 1989)

Evans, M. (1998). Speak the truth to the people. In P. L. Hill (Ed.), *Call and response: The riverside anthology of the African American literary tradition* (p. 1575). (Original work published in 1970)

Fordham, S. (1988). Racelessness as an actor in black students' school success: Pragmatic strategy or pyrrhic victory? *Harvard Educational Review* 58: 54–84.

Foster, M. (1994). The power to know one thing is never the power to know all things: Methodological notes on two studies of Black American teachers. In A. Gitlin (Ed.), *Power and method: Political activism and educational research* (pp. 129–146). New York: Routledge.

Freire, P. (1970). *Pedagogy of the oppressed.* New York: Continuum.

Gibran, K. (1951/2004). *The Prophet.* New York: Alfred A. Knopf.

Giddings, P. (1995). The last taboo. In B. Guy-Sheftall (Ed.), *Words of fire: An anthology of African American feminist thought* (pp. 414–428). New York: The New York Press. (Original work published in 1992)

Giddings, P. (1998). *When and where I enter: The impact of Black women on race and sex in America.* New York: Bantum.

Giroux, H. (1997). *Pedagogy and the politics of hope: Theory, culture, and schooling.* Boulder, CO: Westview Press.

Giroux, H., & Simon, R. (1989). Popular culture and critical pedagogy: Everyday life as a basis for curriculum knowledge. In H. Giroux & P. McLaren (Eds.), *Critical pedagogy, the state and cultural struggle* (pp. 236–252). Albany: State University of New York Press.

Gordon, L. R. (1997a). *Existence in Black: An anthology of Black existential philosophy.* New York: Routledge.

Gordon, L. R. (1997b). *Her majesty's other children: Sketches of racism from a neocolonial age.* Lanham, MD: Rowman & Littlefield.

Gordon, R., Piana, L. D., & Keleher, T. (2000). *Facing the consequences: An examination of racial discrimination in U.S. public schools.* Oakland, CA: Applied Research Center.

Green, M. (1994). The lived world. In L. Stone (Ed.), *The education feminism reader* (pp. 336–348). New York: Routledge. (Original work published in 1978)

Gresson, A. D. (1995). *The recovery of race in America.* Minneapolis: University of Minnesota Press.

Guffy, O. (1971). *The autobiography of a Black woman by Ossie Guffy as told to Gerda Lerner* (1st ed.). New York: Norton.

Guthrie, R. V. (1970). *Being Black: Psychological-sociological dilemmas.* San Francisco: Canfield Press.

Gwaltney, J. L. (1993). *Drylongso: A self-portrait of Black America.* New York: The New York Press.

Hale-Benson, J. (1986). *Black children: Their roots, culture, and learning styles.* Baltimore, MD: Johns Hopkins University Press.

Hale-Benson, J. (1990). Visions for children: Educating black children in the context of their culture. In K. Lomotey (Ed.), *Going to school: The African-American experience* (pp. 209–222). Albany: State University of New York Press.

Hayes, D. L. (1995). *Hagar's daughter: Womanist ways of being in the world.* New York: Paulist Press.

Henry, A. (1993). Missing: Black self-representations in Canadian educational research. *Canadian Journal of Education* 18 (3): 206–222.

Henry, A. (1994). The empty shelf and other curricular challenges of teaching for children of African descent: Implications for teacher practice. *Urban Education* 29 (3): 298–319.

Henry, P. (1997). African and Afro-Caribbean existential philosophies. In L. R. Gordon (Ed.), *Existence in Black: An anthology of Black existential philosophy* (pp. 13–36). New York: Routledge.

hooks, b. (1981). *Ain't I a Woman: Black women and feminism.* Boston: South End Press.

hooks, b. (1989). *Talking back: Thinking feminist, thinking black.* Boston: South End Press.

hooks, b. (1990). Postmodern blackness. http://muse.jhu.edu/journals/postmodern-culture/v001/1.hooks.html

hooks, b. (1993). *Sisters of the yam: Black women and self-recovery*. Boston: South End Press.

hooks, b. (1994). *Teaching to transgress: Education as the practice of freedom*. New York: Routledge.

Jagers, R. J. & Carroll, G. (2002). Issues in the education of African American children and youth. In S. Stringfield and D. Land (Eds.), *Educating at risk students*. Washington, DC: National Society for the Study of Education.

Jewell, K. S. (1993). *From mammy to miss America and beyond: Cultural images and the shaping of US social policy*. New York: Routledge.

Johnson, K. (1997, August 4). Serving superhard time: New prisons isolate worst inmates. *USA TODAY*, 01.A

Jordan-Irving, J. (1990). *Black students and school failure: Policies, practices, and prescriptions*. New York: Greenwood Press.

Joseph, G. (1995). Black feminist pedagogy and schooling in capitalist White America. In B. Guy-Sheftall (Ed.), *Words of fire: An anthology of African American feminist thought* (pp. 462–471). New York: The New York Press. (Original work published in 1988)

Kincheloe, J. (1991). *Teacher as researchers: Qualitative inquiry as a path to empowerment*. New York: Falmer Press.

Kincheloe, J. (2004). *Critical pedagogy primer*. New York: Peter Lang.

Kincheloe, J., & Steinberg, S. (1997). *Changing multiculturalism*. Bristol, PA: Open University Press.

King, D. (1995). Multiple jeopardy, multiple consciousness: The context of a Black feminist ideology. In B. Guy-Sheftall (Ed.), *Words of fire: An anthology of African American feminist thought* (pp. 294–317). New York: The New York Press. (Original work published in 1988)

King, J. E. (1992). Diaspora literacy and consciousness in the struggle against miseducation in the Black community. *Journal of Negro Education* 61(3): 317–340.

King, J. E. (1994a). Being the soul-freeing substance: A legacy of hope and humanity. In M. J. Shujaa (Ed.), *Too much schooling too little education: A paradox of Black life in White societies* (pp. 269–294). Trenton, NJ: Africa Free World Press.

King, J. E. (1994b). Dysconscious racism: Ideology, identity, and miseducation of teachers. In L. Stone (Ed.), *The education feminism reader* (pp. 336–348). New York: Routledge.

King, J. E., & Mitchell, C. A. (1995). *Black mothers to sons: Juxtaposing African American literature with social practice*. New York: Peter Lang.

Kozol, J. (1990). *Savage inequalities: Children in America's schools*. New York: Crown Publishers.

Kunjufu, J. (1984). *Developing positive self-images & discipline in black childen*. Chicago: African-American Images.

Ladson-Billings, G. (1992, Summer). Liberatory consequences of literacy: A case of culturally relevant instruction for African American students. *Journal of Negro Education*, 61(3): 378–391.

Ladson-Billings, G., & Tate, W. F., IV. (1995). Toward a critical race theory of education. *Teachers College Record* 97(1): 47–68.

Lee, C., Lomety, K., & Shujjaa, M. (1990). How shall we sing our sacred song in a strange land? The dilemma of double consciousness and the complexities of an African centered pedagogy. *Journal of Education* 172(2): 45–61.

Lomotey, K. (Ed.). (1991). *Going to school: African-American achievements.* Albany: State University of New York Press.

Lorde, A. (1974). *The brown menace or poem to the survival of roaches. The New York head shop and museum.* Detroit, MI: Broadside.

Lorde, A. (1996a). Eye to eye: Black women, hatred, and anger. In *Sister outsider: Essays & speeches* (11ᵗʰ printing) (pp. 145–175). Freedom, CA: The Crossing Press.

Lorde, A. (1996b). The uses of anger: Women responding to racism. Keynote presentation at the National Women's Studies Association Conference, Storrs, Connecticut, June 1981. In *Sister outsider: Essays & speeches* (11ᵗʰ printing) (pp. 124–133). Freedom, CA: The Crossing Press.

Lorde, A. (1996c). The transformation of silence into language and action. In *Sister outsider: Essays & speeches* (11ᵗʰ printing) (pp. 40–44). Freedom, CA: The Crossing Press.

Madrid, A. (1988). Missing people and others: Joining together to expand the circle. In M. L. Anderson & P. Hill Collins (Eds.), *Race class and gender: An anthology* (2ⁿᵈ Ed.) (pp. 10–15). Belmont, CA: Wadsworth.

McCluskey, A. T. (1997). We specialize in the wholly impossible: Black women school founders and their mission. *Signs: Journal of Women in Culture & Society* 22(2): 403–426.

McKellar, B. (1994). Only the fittest of the fittest will survive: Black women and education. In L. Stone (Ed.), *The education feminism reader* (pp. 229–241). New York: Routledge. (Original work published in 1989)

McLaren, P. (2000). *Che Guevara, Paulo Freire, and the pedagogy of revolution.* Boulder, CO: Rowman & Littlefield.

Moraga, C., & Anzuldula, G. (Eds.). (1981). *This bridge called my back: Radical writings by women of color.* New York: Kitchen Table Women of Color Press.

Murrell, P. C. (1997). Digging again the family wells: A Freirean literacy framework as emancipatory pedagogy for African-American children. In P. Freire, J. W. Fraser, D. Macedo, T. Mckinnon, & W. T. Stokes (Eds.), *Mentoring the mentor: A critical dialogue with Paulo Freire* (pp.19–55). New York: Peter Lang.

Nieto, S. (2000). *Affirming diversity: The sociopolitical context of multicultural education* (3ʳᵈ Ed.). New York: Longman.

Nelson, L. J. Palonsky, B. S., & Carlson, K. (2000). *Critical issues in education: Dialogues and dialectics.* (4ᵗʰ ed.). Boston: McGraw Hill.

Pagano, J. A. (1994). Teaching women. In L. Stone (Ed.), *The education feminism reader* (pp. 252–275). New York: Routledge. (Original work published in 1988)

Patton, M. Q. (1990). *Qualitative evaluation and research methods.* London: Sage.

Pinar, W., Reynolds, W. M., Slattery, P., & Taubman, P. M. (1995). *Understanding curriculum*. New York: Peter Lang.

Pozo, M. (2003). Towards a critical revolutionary pedagogy: An interview with Peter McLaren. *St. John's University Humanities Review*. 2(1). Retrieved April 2004, from http://facpub.stjohns.edu/~ganterg/sjureview/vol2-1/vol2-1.html

Ratteray, J. (1991). African-American achievement: A research agenda emphasizing independent schools. In K. Lomotey (Ed.), *Going to school: The African-American experience* (pp.197–208). Albany: State University of New York Press.

Richardson, L. (1998). Writing: A method of inquiry. In N. K. Denzin & Y. S. Lincoln (Eds.), *Collecting and interpreting qualitative materials* (pp. 345–371). Thousand Oaks, CA: Sage.

Riley, G. (1986). *Inventing the American woman: A perspective on women's history, 1607–1877*. Arlington Heights, IL: Harland Davidson.

Rose, T. (1994). *Black noise: Rap music and black culture in contemporary America*. London: University Press of New England.

Shujja, M. S. (1994). *Too much schooling too little education: A paradox of Black life in White societies*. Trenton, NJ: Africa Free World Press.

Simmons, D. (1962). Possible West African sources for the American Negro dozens. *Journal of American Folklore* 75: 339–340.

Simon, R. I. (1992). *Teaching against the grain: Text for a pedagogy of possibility*. New York: Bergen & Garvey.

Spring, J. (1991). *American education: An introduction to social & political aspect*. Oldwestbury: State College of New York.

Steele, C. M. (1992, April). Race and the schooling of black America. *The Atlantic Monthly*, 68–78.

Sterling, D. (Ed.). (1984). *We are your sisters: Black women in the nineteenth century*. New York: W. W. Norton.

Tatum, B. (2003). *Why are all the Black kids sitting together in the cafeteria? and other conversations about race: A psychologist explains the development of racial identity*, (revised edition). New York: Basic Books.

Vanzant, I. (1995). *The value in the valley: A Black woman's guide through life's dilemmas*. New York: Simon and Schuster.

Wade-Gayles, G. (1984). *No crystal stair: Visions of race and sex in black Women's fiction*. New York: The Pilgrim Press.

Walker, A. (1983). *In search of our mothers' garden: Womanist prose*. San Diego, CA: Harcourt Brace Jovanovich.

Wallace, M. (1995). Anger in isolation: A black feminist's search for sisterhood. In B. Guy-Sheftall (Ed.), *Words of fire: An anthology of African American feminist thought* (pp. 220–230). New York: The New York Press. (Original work published in 1975).

Watkins, W. (1993). Black curriculum orientation. *Harvard Education Review* 63(2): 321–338.

Watkins, W. (2001). *The White architects of Black education: Ideology and power in America, 1865–1954*. New York: Teachers College Press.

Welter, B. (1978). *The cult of true womanhood: 1820–1860. The American family.* In Michael Gordon (Ed.) *The social historical perspective* (pp. 372–392), New York: St. Martin's Press.

White, D. G. (1985). *Aren't I a woman? Female slaves in the plantation south.* New York: W. W. Norton.

Williams, P. (1991). *The alchemy of race and rights: Diary of a law professor.* Cambridge, MA: Harvard University Press.

Wink, J. (1997). *Critical pedagogy: Notes from the real world.* New York: Longman.

Yamato, G. (1995). Something about the subject makes it hard to name. In M. Anderson & P. Hill Collins (Eds.), *Race, class, and gender: An anthology* (pp. 71–75). New York: Wadsworth.

Studies in the Postmodern Theory of Education

General Editors
Joe L. Kincheloe & Shirley R. Steinberg

Counterpoints publishes the most compelling and imaginative books being written in education today. Grounded on the theoretical advances in criticalism, feminism, and postmodernism in the last two decades of the twentieth century, Counterpoints engages the meaning of these innovations in various forms of educational expression. Committed to the proposition that theoretical literature should be accessible to a variety of audiences, the series insists that its authors avoid esoteric and jargonistic languages that transform educational scholarship into an elite discourse for the initiated. Scholarly work matters only to the degree it affects consciousness and practice at multiple sites. Counterpoints' editorial policy is based on these principles and the ability of scholars to break new ground, to open new conversations, to go where educators have never gone before.

For additional information about this series or for the submission of manuscripts, please contact:

Joe L. Kincheloe & Shirley R. Steinberg
c/o Peter Lang Publishing, Inc.
275 Seventh Avenue, 28th floor
New York, New York 10001

To order other books in this series, please contact our Customer Service Department:

(800) 770-LANG (within the U.S.)
(212) 647-7706 (outside the U.S.)
(212) 647-7707 FAX

Or browse online by series:
www.peterlangusa.com